THE ......

By
Lamont Carey

Edited by
Melanee Woodard
Rashidah Denton
Libra Mayo
Lamont Carey

Book Design and graphics
Created by
Leslie "Chuck" McLeod, President, Rap
Ent.

Photo of Lamont Carey taken by
Melanee Woodard

Logo Design by
Kia Kelliebrew

Published by

LaCarey Entertainment, LLC
P.O. Box 64256 Washington, DC 20029

ISBN: 978-0-9816200-5-3

THE WALL

Copyright (C) 2012 by Lamont Carey

www.lacareyentertainment.com
www.lamontcarey.com
Twitter: @lamontcarey

Distributed Worldwide

Special Thanks

Pharaoh, Libra, Penny, Butch, Michelle,
Sheila, Ricardo Burley, Melanee
Woodard, Hermond Palmer, Jr., Felicia
Bass, Dr. Adar Ayira, Robert Garrett,
Brenda Richardson, Natalie Williams,
Tyrone Hicks, Isaac Fulwood, Miranda
Manning, Christine Graham, Salana T,
Leslie "Chuck" Mcloud, SofoReal Ecs
BookClub, Salana, Charles Thornton,
Doc Powell, Yango Sawyer, Marc
Weathers, Kelechi Kalu, Rashidah
Denton, Madam Sec. Hilda Solis, Dr.
Gabriela Lemus, Dr. Cynthia Worsley,
Jahi B. Davis, Kevin Hicks, Kimani
Anku, Afi, The Laws Of The Street Cast,
Sharae Williams, Tinyman, John Blunt,
Andrea Camille, Tom Brown, Wesui,
Monday Childs, Joyce Boston, and my
social network family, my fans, and any
and everyone I forgot.

Dear Reader,

I want to thank you for purchasing this book. It is acts of kindness and support like this that inspires and motivates artists like myself to continue sharing and pursuing their creative passions as this story is the sequel to my first novel "The Hill".

Too often we hear people telling us what we can and cannot accomplish with our lives based on our past. It saddens me that so many of us stop pursuing our dreams because of such negative counsel. NOTHING or NO ONE has the power to direct our destiny unless we give them that power and we determine the outcome by the decisions we make on a daily basis. I learned through mistakes I made in the past, to start making decisions with good intentions and with that good things started happening for me. This book was one of those intentions. I am so thankful and blessed to share with you a story that I created with the hope of enlightening and entertaining the reader!

Whatever you do, I pray you continue to sow into the dreams of others as well as your own. I hope for the opportunity to experience the realization of your dreams. I believe every dream fulfilled makes the world a better place.

Success is my only option! I hope it is yours too!

With much appreciation,

Lamont Carey

P.S. Write me and let me know your thoughts about the book or leave a testimonial on my website: www.lamontcarey.com , email: lacareyentertainment@yahoo.com . Thanks.

Chapter 1

Lighting crackles behind the grey sky. The wind pushes dust through the barbed wire fence that keeps some of DC's deadliest prisoners trapped inside of Lorton. Rehabilitation is almost impossible. A prisoner is more likely to become a killer than a bad guy becoming good. Death happens often. A murder is taking place right now as the thunder shields the screams of the victim. Welcome to THE HILL. The only place scarier than THE HILL is THE WALL.

Chapter 2

"Take a deep breath for me," Dr. Lee tells Sherman while holding his stethoscope against Sherman's bare back, as he listens to his lungs. Sherman is seated on the examining table wearing his institutional light blue khakis and boots. A visibly thick and long scar extends from the bottom left side of his spine to his left shoulder blade. The mark is a reminder from the vicious stabbing by John that left him flatlined.

"Everything sounds good," Dr. Lee says.

"Yea? What's causing the seizures? I never used to have them." Sherman asked with concern.

"Hmm. Your body has experienced serious trauma from that stabbing. Remember your heart was punctured, your left lung collapsed, and you had a lot of tissue damage. You're lucky you survived. It'll take some time before your body feels any normalcy, if at all".

"What kind of damn answer is that?" Sherman snapped.

Dr. Lee glances over to Officer Dexter leaning on the back wall. Sherman glares at Dexter as he walks toward them.

"Mr. Ford, the language isn't necessary," said Dexter.

"That answer is the best I can provide. I can prescribe medication to help prevent them. I offered this to you at least a dozen times before. Would you like something?" Dr. Lee replied.

"No!" Sherman shot back. "I don't want any drugs in me".

Dr. Lee smirks sympathetically.

"Why can't ya send me to a specialist since you don't know the answer to why or how this shit can be stopped?" Sherman snapped.

"A specialist wouldn't be able to provide you any more information than I have already given you," replied Dr. Lee.

With handcuffs on his wrist and shackles on his ankles, Sherman grunts as he eases off of the table, grabbing his shirt beside him. "Ya just don't want to spend the money. Ya rather I died, but I ain't going no damn where but to the streets. I'm ready to go." Sherman barks as he looks at Officer Dexter, showing him the cuffs. "Can you remove these so I can put my shirt on?"

Dexter raises his walkie talkie to his mouth, "Jackson, Ford is ready."

"So, can you give me a medical clearance to return to population?" Sherman asked in a calmer voice.

"I don't see why not, " Dr. Lee responded as muscle bound, baldheaded Sergeant Jackson walked into the room.

"Ford, back against the wall, " Sergeant Jackson barked.

Sherman sighs and does as he is told.

Ten minutes later Sherman is back inside the administrative segregation unit known as "THE HOLE". He is standing on the tier with his palms on the wall outside of his cell door as Officer Dexter unshackles his ankles.

Sergeant Jackson is standing a few feet away daringly watching the back of Sherman. After Officer Dexter removes the last shackle, he takes a few steps back from Sherman and retrieves his walkie talkie. He speaks into his walkie talkie, " Open cell 111".

Sherman turns around and faces Jackson as the cell opens. "Bye-Bye, little jail birdie," Sergeant Jackson says.

Sherman walks into the door as it closes. He throws his arms in the air in disbelief as he sees his tiny cell in shambles with his belongings.

"Ay, Sherman! Ay, Sherman!" Rakeys shouted through the vent above

Sherman's toilet. Rakeys is in the cell next door.

"What?!" Sherman shouts as he pulls his shirt over his head.

"They shook your cell down, Champ!" Rakeys replied.

"I can see that!" Sherman said with a bewildered look on his face.

"Did they find anything? If they did, we can beat that! I already got twenty five dudes off of these fake ass jailhouse beefs and four dudes are on the street now because "I" got their sentences thrown out! Let me know if you need my services!" Rakeys asked.

Sherman is pulling his pants down. There is a six inch shank tied to his inner thigh by strips of a bed sheet. "Naw. I'm good," he says as he grabs one of the ends of the bare plastic mattress dangling off the metal slab that is supposedly the box spring. With a hard push, he shoves the mattress back on the metal slab. He unties the knife and slips it into his hiding place inside of the mattress. He then snatches the sheet from the concrete floor and lays it across the bed.

Sherman sighs as he sits down on the mattress. He looks around at his scattered belongings. He grabs a photograph that is face down on the floor. He brushes the dirt off of it with his index finger as a faint smile surfaces and quickly disappears.

"Hey Ladies," he says to the professional picture of Ella and Loretta. Ella is medium height with a smooth deep dark complexion. She has an hour glass figure with large eyes that match her smile. Loretta is her seven year old mini-me. They are on their knees kissing opposite sides of the ears of a large red teddy bear with a t-shirt on that says, "The World's #1 Dad!"

The slot in the door is unlocked. It slams against the metal door as it opens. "Mail," a male guard's voice shouts from outside the door. Sherman jumps up and grabs three pieces of mail as it appears in the slot. The slot then slams shut.

He smiles as he shuffles through two card size envelopes and a thicker business size envelope. He picks up a tube of toothpaste from the floor beside the toilet, and plops down on the mattress. He sets the envelopes down and unscrews the top of the toothpaste. One dot of toothpaste is placed on his index-finger five separate times, pressing each dot of toothpaste onto the back of the picture. The last dot went in the center. He then presses the picture at the top end of the wall just above the mattress, making the picture stick to the wall like glue. Sherman opens one of the cards. Four pictures of Ella and Loretta fall out onto the mattress. He scans them and reads the front of the card. The front of the card reads: Thinking of you. The inside is handwritten and reads as follow:

"Sherman, I have never known a love more deeper than the one we have. I rarely feel alone even though you have been gone for almost six years now. When loneliness sets in, I either read one of your letters or grab hold of Loretta. You are so blessed.

I don't know if you are aware of how rare you are. You are a man who is capable of such great passion, ambition, and leadership. This is a minor setback for you. You will continue to do amazing things. I just don't want you to ever feel that going to prison makes you a damaged man. I know you don't think like that, but if you ever question your worth, look to me and I will always show you your beauty. I love you with every fiber of my soul. I am so honored you chose me to walk this journey of life with. I will hold your hand until our fingers return to the God we came from. I love you. Your daughter loves you. I'm going to end now. Please don't be mad. I know you just received a six page letter that I wrote, on back and front, and sent yesterday with a card from your daughter. I love you, Sexy. Ella."

He sighs, smiles, and shakes his head. He then smells the card before grabbing the business size envelopes. He opens the envelope as he lies back on the bed underneath the picture on the wall. He reads the rest of his mail before falling off to sleep.

It's 5:00am. Sherman swiftly rolls out of the bed into an attack stance from his deep sleep as his cell door opens with a vibrating metal sound. He stares at the opening door, ready to fight. Sergeant Jackson fills the doorway. Two other guards are standing behind him. Other guards can be seen walking pass the cell toward other cells.

"What in the hell have you done to this cell?" Jackson barks as he signals toward the ransacked cell.

"Ya did that when ya shook down my cell yesterday, " Sherman replied.

"Trifling. Pack up! You're being sent to lovers lane," Jackson said humorously.

"What?" Sherman questioned.

"You're being transferred to The Wall. I'll be back in five minutes," Jackson replied.

The guards step out the cell. The door closes. Sherman relaxes.

"Hey, Sherman! You aight over there?" Rakeys shouts through the vent.

"They sending me to The Wall," Sherman shouted back as he begins to untie his sheet and starts putting his belongings inside of the sheet.

"Damn!! Look, Sherman, I heard that spot is vicious! They be trying to get motherfuckers pregnant over there! Watch your back!" Rakeys says with concern.

Sherman can hear some banging on Rakeys door.

"Get your ass off that toilet before I pop your cell," Sergeant Jackson barks.

"You better bring a motherfucking army with you! Ain't nothing but a gangster in here," Rakeys shouts.

Chapter 3

Sherman is seated three rows from the back of the prison bus next to a young man in an orange prison jumpsuit. Both of their hands and ankles are shackled along with the other eighteen prisoners on the bus. The young African American man seated beside him is of average height and build with a cream colored complexion and seawater blue eyes.

Sherman appears as if he is looking straight ahead but he is actually counting the number of men on the bus in orange prison jumpsuits. He counts twelve total with eight men including himself wearing Lorton's light blue pants, shirts and jackets. One White guy and four Latino men stand out in this crowd amongst the varying skin tones of Black men.

Sergeant Jackson stands up from his seat opposite the bus driver. He goes and grips the cage door that separates them from the prisoners.

"Mr. Ford, I know you're happy to be off PC, " he barks.

Sherman doesn't respond. All of the prisoners start looking at the guy seated next to them and then at the people behind them. Sherman keeps looking straight but the young man seated next to him glances at him.

Sergeant Jackson unlocks the cage door and steps in. He locks himself inside the cage with the prisoners before walking towards and towering over top of Sherman.

"Mr. Ford, I know you're glad to be off of protective custody. Then again, I'm sure you don't want to go behind The Wall. I know you heard the stories of what they do to fresh meat back there,' Sergeant Jackson yells.

Sherman keeps looking straight ahead. "So, I was on PC, uh"?

"You weren't in population," Sergeant Jackson yells.

"So, you're trying to tell these dudes that I got [1]checked in," Sherman says in the most controlled voice he could muster.

"Actually, I'm talking to you! I know you don't care what they think because you think you're a bad ass. That's why they damn near killed you on The Hill," Sergeant Jackson snapped.

Sherman's leg starts to rock as he lowers his head to conceal his rage.

"Hopefully, you learned you're not as bad as you thought you were," Sergeant Jackson said in a softer but loud voice. Then he walks out of the gate and locks it behind him. He grabs the shotgun and sits back down. "We'll be arriving in a few minutes. Take a good look, Gentlemen. Some of you will never see this side of the wall again".

---

[1] *CHECK IN means to be placed in a cell and housing area away from all other prisoners. It is also known as PC or protective custody.*

"Asshole," the young man, Blue Eyes, seated next to Sherman whispers. "Cuzzo, are all the guards down here like that?" he asks.

Sherman looks straight ahead before sighing, "Naw. You have a few of them smelling themselves, but most of them mind their business."

"Cool. That's fucked up he put your business in the air, Cuzzo."

Sherman doesn't respond. A young, tall, and slender guy seated in front of Sherman, wearing the Lorton uniform, stares back at him. "That was some bitch ass shit he said. I know you wanted to put that knife in him," Yesterday said, visibly upset.

Sherman doesn't respond. He looks down the aisle.

"By the way, my name is Yesterday," The slender man adds.

Sherman nods his head as if he is listening to music.

"Yesterday? How did you get the name Yesterday, Cuzzo?" Asks Blue Eyes.

"Because yesterday is the last time you see a dude if he gets in my business. What's ya name? And who the fuck is Cuzzo. It sure ain't me!" Yesterday responded.

"My fault. No disrespect intended. I call everybody Cuzzo. But I'm Blue Eyes. Self explanatory, right?" Blue Eyes replies pointing to his eyes.

"What's your name?" Yesterday directs to Sherman.

Sherman looks him in his eyes, "Sherman."

Blue Eyes and Yesterday nod their heads in agreement.

"Excuse me, Men. Well, this question is more to the two guys in the Lorton blues," says the guy seated next to Yesterday.

Sherman looks at him with very little interest. Yesterday looks eager.

"Wussup?" Yesterday asks.

"First, my name is Butch. Look, I have never been locked up before but I got five to fifteen years. I was at the jail for over four and a half years of that. I supposed to see the parole board in a couple of months. I'm trying to make parole the first time up. How do I do my time and not get caught up in anything?"

Blue Eyes is looking eagerly at Yesterday and Sherman for answers.

"Butch, just mind your business. Don't borrow. Don't steal. Don't gamble. Don't sell shit and don't fuck with homosexuals. If you mind your business, you should be aight. Whatever you do always keep your boots on and tied tight. You wear them even in the shower because you never know when shit is going to get drastic," Sherman sincerely said.

"Sheeit. The first thang you have to do is put that knife in the first mothafucka that disrespects you. Once you do that, they'll stay out of your business. Why they sending you to The Wall and all you have is five to fifteen years? I got life plus 30 years," Yesterday questioned.

"Yea because I have forty years to life, Cuzzo," Blue Eyes blurted.

"I took a plea to twenty-five years to life for shooting a cop. The judge gave me that but suspended all but five to fifteen years." Butch politely replied.

"Something don't sound too mothafuckkun right about that? You told on a muthafucka?" Yesterday asks with a sinister stare.

Anger flares in his eyes but disappears immediately. "Tell on who? I'm not hot. A plains clothed cop ran down on me in my car. He was screaming with a gun in his hand. I didn't know what he was saying, so I started shooting. I hit him four times. The judge gave me leniency because it was broad daylight and a lot of people wrote statements that he didn't identify himself," Butch says calmly.

"Damn! You go hard! You tried to [2]smash a cop! You'll be alright in this joint, Cuzzo," Blue Eyes said gleefully.

Yesterday nods his approval.

"How old are you?" Butch asks.

"I'm seventeen, Cuzzo," Blue Eyes says smiling.

"Dag. You seventeen with forty years to life," Butch says as he and Yesterday shake their heads.

"I'm good. I'ma give all of this time back. How old are you, Cuzzo?" Blue Eyes questions.

"I'm one year older than you are," Butch replies.

"Here is The Wall as you all call it! Just so you'll know. This facility was built between 1935-1940 and The Wall is 55 feet tall. There are seven cell blocks behind this wall," Sergeant Jackson

---

[2] *note: SMASH means to kill someone. "You tried to smash a cop?".*

grabs a clipboard and scans the contents on the top page. "It appears you all are going to The Houses of Pain. We call it cell block one, two and three. Here ya will be mixed in with the worse of the worse and the mentally ill. This should be exciting for you all," he laughs. "Now is a good time to check in. Mr. Ford, are you good?" he says as he continues to laugh.

Sherman sighs and lowers his head. The rest of the men, except Blue Eyes, stare out of the window at the huge dirty wall that seems to reach the clouds. Their thoughts are mixed. Some realize the Sergeant was right in the fact that they will never see this side of the wall again. Some have flash backs of times with their loved ones. The others envision violent scenes that will take place behind this notorious place.

"Bitch ass nigga. I'm surprised nobody hasn't put that knife in him, Cuzzo," Blue Eyes said about Sergeant Jackson.

"I forgot to add, there is no escape," Sergeant Jackson said, as the bus stops at the security entrance. Sergeant

Jackson hands the clipboard to the driver.

The security doors at the entrance, are dark and hugely intimidating. They resemble medieval castle doors. As the doors screeched open, the bus enters. The door closes behind them. There is another pair of matching doors in front of the bus and a guard booth off to the side. Lieutenant (LT.) Morgan and Sergeant Gant exit the booth. Sergeant Gant has a metal stick device that has a mirror on the end of it. He begins searching underneath the bus for anything unusual, like weapons or prisoners trying to escape.

The bus door opens and Lieutenant Morgan steps onto the bus. He shakes Jackson's hand. The driver hands him the clipboard. "We have twenty for you," Sergeant Jackson says to Lt. Morgan. Morgan nods his approval as he walks over to the cage door.

"Listen up!! And sit up if you are asleep. I need to count you and I need you to hear what I have to tell you," he says as he counts the men. "My name is Lieutenant Morgan. I want to unfortunately welcome you to Lorton's maximum security prison. I'm sure most of you will be here longer than others. I know you're angry. However, I had nothing to do with your sentencing. None of the guards here had anything to do with your case. I don't care what you did to get here. My job is to make sure you do your time. With that being said, I don't want any problems out of you and you won't have any problems out of us. When you get on my compound, I suggest you mind your business. You may see some of your buddies from your old neighborhood. I advise you not to immediately start hanging out with them. They are no longer the same people you knew from better times in your lives. Plus, if you start running around with them before you become familiar with their situations in here, you could end up dead. Their beefs become your beefs even if you don't know the beefs exist. The person or persons they are having issues with don't care if you're new. I advise you again, mind your own business. Now, we have plenty of assholes in here and plenty of killers. When those two collide someone is going to die. We are trying hard to stop it, but we have had forty murders a year for the last four years and there are only twenty of you on this bus. Some of you are not going to listen to me and end up dead. Mind your business, Gentlemen. I want to inform you now that we have cameras all over the compound except for inside the cell blocks. So, if you get killed in the block, we won't have a clue as to who murdered you unless one of your fellow prisoners comes forward, but that rarely happens. So, if you're a fuck up, do us a favor and get killed on the compound, that way we'll see it. Also, we have a protective custody unit. All of the inmates call it PC. If you are interested in going to the PC unit, say something to me when you get off the bus. I can't stress it enough- mind your business here. Now there is a law library back there. Try to work on your case so you can hopefully go home one day. Another thing, you are all men. This is the perfect time to start being one. We do not tolerate horse playing. Horse playing can get you sent to the hole or even worse, killed. You are going to the worse housing units on the compound. The cells you will be living in became available for you because the last person was either murdered or is in the hole for murdering the person from one of the other cells that one of you will be moving into. People rarely go home here. This is the last stop before going to the grave, Gentlemen. Again, this is not a playground. You are going to the worse housing units and I say it's the worse because it's where most of the bad shit happens. Mind your business men, and you'll get along just fine," Lt. Morgan strongly suggested.

The bus gets deathly quiet as it enters the compound. The heartbeats of every prisoner is blocking out every sound as fear, the feeling of death and the unknown send their thoughts racing with frightening images. Their eyes don't even blink as they remain glued to the window hoping for or fearing some of the horror stories they have heard from others on the street and in other prisons about how men die horrible deaths behind The Wall.

As the bus turns left on the narrow road that wraps around the outskirts of the cell blocks, they only have a partial view of the seven cell blocks on their right. The cell blocks resemble the fronts of churches if it wasn't for the metal bars on the windows.

As the bus pulls up to the Receiving building, an ambulance is visibly and awkwardly parked at the back of Cell Block Two. The lights are flashing. Eight guards appear, escorting two handcuffed men out of the side door of Cell Block Two. One of the men is shirtless with blood drying on his flesh and his pants. It's not his blood. He is being escorted by two guards. The other man is resisting and six guards struggle to keep him within their grip. His white t-shirt is ripped and stretched. The rest of his body is drenched in blood. The blood isn't his own.

A few seconds later, four medics come swiftly out of the cell block pushing a man lying lifeless on a stretcher toward the ambulance. One of the medics is desperately trying to *revive the man with hard presses against his chest. Blood covers the man's upper body, the medics arms, and blood spots are seeping through the white sheet that covers the dying man's lower body. The man was stabbed two hundred times and one of his eyeballs was sliced in half. The attack happened because he failed to repay one of his attackers a pack of cigarettes that he owed him.*

"It appears that three more cells have just opened up in Cell Block Two. I will be reassigning a few of you to that cell block. Gentlemen, that is Cell Block Two," Lt. Morgan says as he points to the block where the ambulance is parked. He then scans the clipboard. "Mr. Butch Lawrence, Mr. Albert Marshall, Mr. Floyd Davison, Mr. Eric Mitchell, Mr. Ronald Washington, Mr. Jose Daiz, Mr. Raul Negron, Skip Donavon, and Mr. Miles White, raise your hands."

Yesterday, Butch, Blue Eyes, and several other men scattered around the bus including the white guy raised their hand. Each man immediately scans the area to see who else is being called.

"You all will be going to Cell Block Two," Lt. Morgan informed.

The men whose names were called stopped breathing for a few seconds. The others sighed in relief except Sherman and two other men.

Lt. Morgan continues to call off names for other cell blocks.

"Dag. I have to go to that joint. They already killing folks. Dag," Butch said with regret.

"Shit. I have to go in that joint, too. It's whateva, Cuzzo," Blue Eyes says encouraging himself.

"That's what's up! My man is over there too. I'm good! Either way, I'ma put my knife in the first dude that jumps out there!" Yesterday boasts.

"Damn. Cuzzo, I wish you were going with us. You seem like a really laid back and cool dude," Blue Eyes says to Sherman.

"Just be a man, Shawty, and you'll be good," Sherman replies.

"Will the following men raise your hand", Lt. Morgan shouts as the bus stops in front of the larger building. "Mr. Donald Reeks raise your hand".

Donald is a muscular black man with plaits. He's wearing Lorton blues. He raises his hand from his seat on the left side of the bus in the front row by the cage door.

"Mr. Enrique Gomez, raise your hand," Lt. Morgan shouts.

A slender Latino man in the middle row on the left raises his hand.

"And Mr. Sherman Ford, raise your hand," Lt. Morgan requests.

Sherman raises his hand.

"Yes, Cuzzoooo" Blue Eyes shouts.

Sherman just stares at him.

"You three will be reassigned to Cell Block Two. Again, men, that is the unit where the ambulance is skidding off from now. You can not request to be transferred from a cell block before you enter it. However, you can refuse to enter the block and you will be placed on protective custody. Just ask to speak with me as you file off the bus. If you don't wish to speak to me, just exit the bus and stop in front of that building at the curb. That is the building right here, " Lt. Morgan says, while pointing in the direction of the building. "Ok. Left side stand and file out in the order that you are seated," he says as he opens the cage and walks off the bus.

Sergeant Jackson cocks the shotgun, stares at them, then exits the bus. The driver follows him.

Blue Eyes, Butch, and Yesterday exit the bus before Sherman.

"Bitch ass niggas," Yesterday blurts in disgust toward the six men standing behind Lt. Morgan. One of the men is Donald.

"From Mr. Marshall on back stop for a second," Lt. Morgan calmly asks.

Butch stops. Yesterday and all the men behind him including the two men behind Sherman stop. Lt. Morgan looks Yesterday straight in his eyes, " Mr. Eric Mitchell, don't be surprised if you don't find yourself over here tomorrow," Lt. Morgan tells him.

"Sheed. I came in a man and I'ma leave one!" Yesterday snaps.

"Your definition of being a man isn't correct. I hope you didn't ruin your life thinking hurting people is what makes you a man," Lt. Morgan says sorrowfully. "Now Mr. Ronald Washington, Mr. Sherman Ford, Mr. Albert Marshall, Mr. Butch Lawrence, and you, Mr. Eric Mitchell, I want you all to go stand beside those four men behind Sergeant Jackson. We have to lock ya down until things get sorted out in the block."

Sergeant Morgan looks at the clipboard then gestures toward the cell block each man in front of him is assigned to. Some of the men are already in route.

"Excuse me, Lt. Morgan; I would like to have a word with you," said one of the men behind Sherman.

"Step over here with these other men behind me, Mr. Ronald Washington," Lt. Morgan causally replies. Ronald does as he is told.

"I can't believe this shit," Yesterday says laughing.

Chapter 4

Sunlight peeks over the prison wall. The air is cozy. Fourteen correctional officers float around on the compound grounds. Seven of them are walking toward the main building as their work day comes to an end. The others are walking to the cell blocks as their workday begins. The nine prisoners who were assigned to Cell Block Two exit the main building wearing the Lorton uniform with black boots. Each man is carrying a bed roll consisting of a blanket, two sheets, three pair of underwear, a pair of light blue pants, another sky blue shirt, a sky blue jacket and a zip lock size bag that contains a small tube of toothpaste, one toothbrush, one bar of soap, one washcloth and one stick of deodorant all rolled up in the blanket.

"Man, them bamas kept us locked down for three days!!" Yesterday shouted with displeasure.

"I heard it was another stabbing in Cell Block One, Cuzzo. They said it was one of the new dudes that came down with us. They said he wasn't going to make it, Cuzzo," Blue Eyes confided.

Butch shakes his head. "Dag. He just got down here. That's crazy," he said.

"The first thing ya better do is make ya a knife. That's my main priority," Yesterday warns.

"I don't know how to do that, Cuzzo," Blue Eyes admits.

"I'll show you, Shawty; we family. I gotcha," Yesterday replies.

Blue Eyes nods his approval.

"My first priority is getting out of here as soon as possible," Butch firmly states.

Skip Donavon is walking ahead of the pack. He is the only white guy that came on the bus with them. Yesterday, Blue Eyes, Butch and Sherman are a few feet behind him. They follow Skip to the side door of Cell Block Two. He knocks on the door. A few seconds later a buzzer goes off. Skip pulls the door open. Three of the men file in behind him. They are boxed in by the two large connecting gates that leaves only enough room for Skip, Yesterday, Sherman, and Butch to fit in. Blue Eyes steps back into the open door way.

Sherman scans the area. He sees Sergeant Jackson looking over his right shoulder at them from his seat behind the single desk. They are facing the tiers on the other side of the gate where he has a clear view of the four tiers. Two of the tiers are stacked on top of each other. The tiers are on each corner of the far wall. The tiers on top are identified as A Upper and B Upper. The tiers beneath share the same A or B tier identification but these are labeled as A Lower and B Lower. The tiers are narrow with a long walkway that stretches from the back shower area to the dual entrance/exit door.

Each side has its own entrance and exit. A and B are separated by a 10 by 20 foot brick wall and the guard station's gate. A walking trail has been created to enter/exit the bottom of A and

B tiers that leads to gated partitions on each side, three feet from the exit/enter doors to the unit. However, there is no trail where the prisoners can walk from A tier to B tier. Those on upper tiers have to enter and exit the area from the lower tiers. They have to travel through the shower area at the back of the lower tiers to get to a staircase that leads to and from the upper areas. There is no way the prisoners living on A and B tiers can co-mingle inside the unit.

The Sergeant's area resembles a large cage within the exit doors and the tiers. It's designed to keep prisoners from entering, especially during a riot. A switchboard is located near the exit doors but on the inside of the cage. It is used to unlock all doors, cells and gates in the unit. All of the prisoner's cell doors are made of bars, leaving them without privacy. Anyone can walk up to the cell and see directly inside.

Sherman lifts his chin and can now see on B upper in the distance. No one is on the tier, but he can see the first four cells on the right side of the tier. The cell doors are open. B lower is in plain view. There are cells along the left side of the tier and a brick wall on the right side. He spots Psycho, a muscular bald headed Aryan Brother walking towards them. He has on a t-shirt that barely covers his muscles. Tattoos cover all of his visible flesh and there are six tear drop tattoos that appear to be falling from the corner of his left eye and three from the corner of his right eye. In between his eye is a tattoo that reads 666.

Sherman looks past Psycho. B Lower seems dimly lit, but fully visible and narrow. The place has a damp feel. The walkway is only wide enough for Psycho to walk through. His shoulders nearly touch the wall and the cell bars. He sees Suga and Veins at the back of the tier. Veins has on a long sleeve shirt and pants. Suga is a full-figured homosexual, usually in a tight t-shirt with the bottom left end tied. His belly fat hangs over his belt. His pants are extremely tight fitting. He is leaning against the wall and Veins is leaning against his cell. He is barely visible but his upper body keeps dropping forward as he laughs. Suga stares down at the *new prisoners. Veins reaches out for Suga's hand but he pulls away.*

Psycho stops at the gate near the exit doorway. He stares straight into Skip's eyes. "Hey Brother," he says.

Skip looks quizzically at him before nodding his head.

"Did you just come from the jail?" Psycho asked.

Sergeant Jackson shoves his chair backwards as he leaps up, "Get back on your tier! Now!" He grabs a clipboard and pen off of the desk before threateningly walking over toward Psycho. He stops at the gate that separates them.

"Ok, Sergeant. Just make sure you put him on my tier. Please, Sir," Psycho says sarcastically. "I'll see you in a few minutes, Brother."

Sergeant Jackson stares at Psycho until he walks back on B Lower and leans on the wall near the walkway.

"You know him?" Sergeant Jackson asks.

Skip shakes his head no.

"I advise you to stay clear of him. He's bad news," Sergeant Jackson says.

Sherman spots Veins handing something to Suga but he can't make out what it is. Suga looks briefly at it before walking into Veins' cell.

"Mr. Ford, welcome to Cell Block Two," Sergeant Jackson says, smiling, "As you can see, both of us have been transferred."

Sherman smirks.

"Now you fools in the doorway, either close the door or gather around in the doorway. Don't mind touching each other. I will not repeat myself," Sergeant Jackson snaps.

The men come in closer but not as close as he suggested. Sergeant Jackson points to Butch, "What's your name?"

"Butch Lawrence," he replies.

"You're going to B-18," Jackson says before pointing to Yesterday in the doorway. "What's your name?" he asks him.

"Eric Mitchell."

"Ok. You sleep in upper B-21. That's on the upper tier up there. You have to walk through B lower all the way through the back of the tier and through the other side of the shower. You'll see the flight of stairs. That's your cell right there," Jackson says, pointing to the cell right above Lower B.

After Sergeant Jackson informs them of their cells, he hits the switch and the gate opens. The new prisoners walk onto the tiers. Blue Eyes walks into Lower B-5 with his bed roll under his arm. Big Bob is reading the newspaper from a seated position on the bottom bunk inside the two man cell. He looks up from his newspaper at Blue Eyes with very little interest. "You my new celly?" he asks.

"Yea, Cuzzo," Blue Eyes replies.

The gigantic muscle bound Big Bob smiles a welcoming smile as he stands. He quickly folds his mattress. "Who in the fuck is Cuzzo?"

"No disrespect. I call everybody that, " Blue Eyes says.

"Ya kids today always renaming somebody," Big Bob says, smiling, " Well, take that mattress up there and put it down here," he says.

"I'm good. I can sleep up there, Cuzzo," Blue Eyes replies.

"Naw, Kid. I only sleep down here when I don't have a cell buddy. Plus, I'm getting old. I need the exercise. So, I insist. What's your name?" He questions as Blue Eyes moves the mattress to the bottom bunk.

"Albert Marshall, but my friends call me Blue Eyes, Cuzzo," he says.

Big Bob starts smiling.

Chapter 5

Rocket is leaning on the toilet and sink combo near the exit door of his cell. He is watching Butch make up his bed on the top bunk. " That's not a long time. Shit. I have 175 years," Rocket says. Rocket is a muscular light-skinned man in his early 50's with graying hair. "How old are you?"

"Eighteen," Butch replied.

"Yea. Five to fifteen years is not a long time. You can make parole the first time up. It's rare but it has happened. I was eighteen when I came to prison," Rocket replies with a ton of anguish in his voice.

"Really? How old are you now?" Butch replied in astonishment.

"Fifty five. I turned fifty five last month on May 5th," he said shaking his head in disbelief. "I'm old. Good thing you'll make it out of here a young man. You just have to stay out of these fools way. The best advice I can give you is to keep your distance from everyone and always mind your business. And as far as everybody else is concerned, you don't have no business. These fools will search for weaknesses in you. They'll ask about your family, how much time you got, what you in for, you got any girls you can hook them up with, and if they can borrow something. You just politely tell them, 'All that is irrelevant. These fools will exploit you, embarrass you, and try to kiss you in the mouth if you don't stand firm. Now standing firm doesn't mean killing one of these fools. It means letting them know you ain't scared but you don't want no problems. However, one of these fools is going to try you. You fight for your life, but don't kill'em because you'll just replace him if he had a life sentence. Now go on and get yourself together. We have enough time to talk," he says as he walks out of the cell.

Butch smiles and continues to make his bed.

Chapter 6

Skip is seated on the edge of the top bunk. He is looking at Larry, his cell buddy, who is standing in front of him and staring him in his eyes. Larry is a muscular light skinned black man with curly hair and gray eyes.

"So you came all the way from Annapolis, Maryland to kill a motherfucking black man," Larry barks.

"I killed a man who decided it was easier to rob me than to give me the drugs I came to purchase from him. It wasn't about his color," Skip calmly responds.

"I'm not comfortable with that. That shit doesn't sound right. How many Black people have you killed?" Larry says as Skip eases off of the bed and stares non-threateningly into Larry's eyes.

"I don't want any problems with you, but I don't appreciate the way you coming off to me," Skips says.

Larry makes his chest muscles jump as he loosens his neck and balls his fist. "So, you want to kill me too, cracker?" Larry says.

Skip takes a few steps away from him. "Again, I don't want no problems, man. I just want to do my time."

"Then you don't be jumping your sucker ass off the bed like you ready to go to war with a war hero," Larry says as he makes his chest muscles jump again.

Chapter 7

There are amazing pencil drawings pasted along the wall above the top bunk. Pictures of Nelson Mandela, Michael Jordan leaping through the air, a voluptuous black woman, Bob Marley, a knight slaying a dragon, and a picture of an open cell door that leads to a sunny road with footprints in the street.

Yesterday's cell buddy, BH Bandit is watching him as he makes his bottom bunk when Black Smoke appears in their cell door with Dre and Marc. "Yesterday!" Black Smoke barks. Yesterday and his cell buddy look to them. Black Smoke is not smiling. A smile slowly blossoms on Yesterday's face, "Wusssssssup, Bl-ack Smoke," he shouts as he swiftly walks toward him. Black Smoke frowns and steps back.

"Let me holla at you out here for a minute,You know what I'm saying," Black Smoke says as he licks his lips and rubs his hands. A quizzical look comes over BH Bandit and Yesterday's face. Yesterday hunches his shoulder and follows him onto the tier. The men have him boxed in. Neither man is smiling at him.

"Smoke, wussup, man! You don't seem excited to see me," Yesterday says jokingly. BH Bandit is seated on his bed eavesdropping.

"Man, I ain't happy to see you. You know what I am saying. What have you done for me? You know what I am saying. I got 62 years on a body we did. You know what I am saying. I ate that beef by myself. You know what I am saying. You were my man and you ain't send me a dime. You know what I am saying. You ain't even send me one card, go see my mother or nothing. You know what I am saying. And you want me to be happy to see you? You know what I am saying," he said in anger as he continues to rub his hands and lick his lips.

Yesterday's smile vanishes. He glances around at the two men with him and then locks his stare on Black

Smoke's eyes. "Hold up. You coming at me like that?" he barks.

"Like what? You know what I am saying" Black Smoke replies with less hostility.

Yesterday looks at the two men with Black Smoke, "Like this. What ya coming to [3]'put some work in?'" Yesterday says visibly irritated. Dre and Marc lock eyes on him. They're ready to follow whatever lead Black Smoke takes.

"Hold up. Hold up. Ain't nobody coming at you like nothing! You know what I am saying. I was just letting you know how you treated me was fucked up. You know what I am saying. Now I see you, and you're smiling in my face. You know what I am saying," He replied with the same aggression as Yesterday. He starts licking his lips and rubbing his hands again.

---

[3] *Note: "Put some work in" means to have the intentions of hurting or killing someone.*

"So, what's up? Are we still family or we got issues?" Yesterday barks.

"Yesterday, we good. You know what I am saying," Black Smoke replies with less hostility.

"Ok. Well, I need to be strapped ASAP," Yesterday replies.

"Ok. Lets walk. I'll arm you now. You know what I am saying," Black Smoke says before peeping in Yesterday's cell, "Yea. You have to watch Mr. BH Bandit. You know what I am saying," he says as they head down the tier.

"Why you say that?" Yesterday asks.

"BH stands for butt hole. He is a butt hole bandit. It's like four of them that be running around here raping dudes," Black Smoke replies.

Chapter 8

Skip is shaking the hand of two Rambo size, baldheaded and tattooed covered Aryan Brothers as Psycho shakes his head in approval. The men are all standing on the side of the showers.

"Nice to meet you, Brother," said Razor to Skip. Razor is the shorter of the four men. He has bright green eyes that appear to glow and a bald head with a swastika tattoo above each ear. There are three tear drop tattoos that look like falling tears from the corner of his left eye. He also has a thick scar that runs from his left eyebrow to the corner of the right side of his lip. There is a thicker scar that runs from one side of his neck across his adam's apple to the other side of his neck.

Bear is the other man. He looks like a wrestler. He has short bright red hair that is cut military style and six tear drop tattoos that look like fallen tears from the corner of his left eye. There is a swastika tattoo on top of his adam's

apple and on the back of both of his
hands. He stares Skip in his eyes. His
large hands are on his waist.

"Brother, we are a unit. If one of us goes
somewhere, majority of the time, we all
go. These niggers and spics are
savages and they will try to pounce on
the superior race. This is why we stick
together. If one of them niggers or spics
bothers any of us, they feel the full
extent of white power rain down on their
asses. For the most part we don't have
too many problems until new niggers or
spics come down here. They think all
white boys are punks. They know not to
fuck with us. This is why we are coming
to you, Brother, you won't make it 72
hours without a black dick in your ass or
getting your throat cut. Now if they know
you are with us, you won't have any
problems. What you say? Are you
becoming a part of the Brotherhood?"
Psycho asks.

"I'm not a racist. I don't want any
problems or get mixed up in any gangs,"
Skip says. They then pause as Suga
and another homosexual by the name of
Nancy walks down the stairs into the

shower area. They look at the glaring Aryans with suspicion as they walk out onto the lower tier switching.

Bear stands nose to nose with Skip, "Are you a nigger lover? You got you one of those ape whores? Only nigger lovers don't understand the sensitivity of their situation. Boy, if you ain't with us, we shipping your ass out of here right fucking now," Bear threatens.

Skip balls his fist. Psycho grabs Skip's wrist as he steps in between the two men. He looks Skip in his eyes, "Brother, this is a delicate situation. You have 54 years. You won't survive in here alone. Don't think if you play nice that one of these niggers ain't going to come for you. Let me tell you about these animals. All the niggers want is some dope, some butt-holes, and some knives. They use the knives to get the other two. Soon they'll come for your ass and to make you call home to get money to buy them dope. The spics want assholes and knives. This place is filled with a bunch of faggots. Are you one?" Psycho questions.

"Hell no," Skip barks.

Psycho reassuringly places his hand on Skip's shoulder, " My Brother, if you don't join us, we're going to have to fuck you up real bad in here. We can't leave you to them. That will disgrace us all. Plus, that will make them come after us once they turn you into a nice piece of ass. We can't have that. We're only thirty deep on this compound and it is two hundred and fifty of them. You have to make a decision. If you think you can make it on your own, you're all the way on your own. Ain't no coming back to us once the shit hits the fan," Psycho steps back and the three men stare at Skip as he stares at them. Bear is rubbing his fist.

Chapter 9

Sherman stops and scans the visiting room from the inmate entrance. As he hands his pass to the guard seated near the door, he sees that there are thirteen square tables positioned around the center of the room. Each table has three chairs. Two chairs face a single chair across the table. There are only two other prisoners in the visiting room. The two men are seated on opposite ends of the room with their visitor. One man has his head lowered as his father is desperately trying to encourage him to stay focused, remain positive, and that God will deliver him when he is ready to be free. The other man is leaning over the table and wiping the tears from his wheelchair-bound and overweight mother's cheeks. She has a tube from her portable oxygen tank in her nose. He is trying to calm down her breathing by reassuring her that she will not die before he is released. The guard walks over and compassionately reminds the prisoner that he can only touch his visitor at the beginning and at the conclusion of the visit.

"But she's crying," the prisoner calmly says.

"I understand. What I can do is give her some tissue," the guard suggested.

"No, I'll be fine, Sir. Thank you, anyway," the elderly woman says.

"If you change your mind, just wave me over. Mr. Hardy, you have twenty more minutes before your visit ends. Enjoy the rest of the visit," the guard says before walking back over to his desk near the door that Sherman entered.

Sherman spots Corporal Susan leaning over in between Ella and Loretta. Loretta is telling Susan a story that happened in her second grade class. Both women are enjoying the story. Susan looks up and waves him over to the table. He walks toward them. Loretta spots him, leaps up, and runs into his arms, "Daddy! Daddy!" she shouts as he whisks her into the air before planting a big kiss on the four corners of her face. "Awww. Daddy! You're wetting my face, Da-ddy!"

"I can't kiss you? You're too big for Daddy to kiss you?" he says laughing.

"Yessssss, you can, Da-ddy. Mommy and I went to the other place and you weren't there. They told us they moved you here so Mommy drove fast all the way over here," she gushes.

"Girl, you tell all mommy's business," Ella says as she stands to hug and kiss him.

Susan lips twist into a half smirk.

After Ella releases him, she notices the awkward moment between Susan and Sherman. Susan was leaning in for a hug while he motioned for a handshake. They end up doing neither.

"Hello, Mr. Ford. I wasn't aware you were here until I saw Ella and the adorable Ms. Loretta," Susan says.

Loretta giggles.

"Yea. I been here for three days. I just got on the compound," he says with very little interest in talking to her.

"What cell block are you in?" Susan asks.

"Cell Block 2," he dryly replies.

"Ok. Well, I don't want to eat up your visiting time," she says as Ella stands and hugs her.

"Girl, give me a call," Ella says.

"Will do. Bye, Ms. Loretta," Susan says.

Loretta jumps up and wraps her arms around Susan's waist. Susan smiles as she looks into Sherman's eyes. He is not pleased.

"Bye-bye, Aunt Susan," Loretta says.

"I'll say bye to you all before you leave," Susan says before walking away.

Sherman hugs Ella again before directing her to sit. He sits on the opposite side of the table.

"Why did they move you here? Are you ok?" Ella says with concern.

"Yea. I don't know why they moved me. They do stuff like that," he confides.

"But this is maximum security. I thought they move people here when they have been in trouble," she says.

"Look, I guess they moved me because of the incident before I went to the hole. How are you? Is everything ok at home?" he asks.

"Yes. Everything is good. I sent you two hundred dollars yesterday but I sent it to the other address. Will you get it or should I send you some more money? I mean, I can't send two hundred but I may be able to send fifty dollars, then when the other money comes back, I'll send you one hundred and fifty dollars back," she informs.

"I'll check. Have you spoken to "E?" he says.

"Sherman, I hope you're done with that. You have a good chance of making parole this time. I don't want you to keep taking these risks. We need you home. I only come here because we don't have a choice. I don't want Loretta, myself, or you in here. So, please, stop. I got a raise so I can send you money," she pleads.

"All I asked was did you speak to him," he says smiling.

She reaches out and caresses his hand.

"Mommy, you know you can't touch Daddy until the end of the visit now. We don't want Daddy to get in trouble," Loretta says with fear.

He reaches over and rubs her head, "It's ok," he says as he sighs.

"See. You see this? She knows the rules of the prison," Ella says tearfully.

Chapter 10

Blue Eyes and Yesterday are standing on opposite sides of Butch. He's standing in the door way of his cell. Rocket isn't in the cell.

"Excuse me, Gentlemen," Suga says. He blushes at them as he makes his behind shake when he passes them. He scans back at them only to see each man frowning. He then laughs, "In time, Gentlemen, in time".

"If he ever say something slick to me, I'ma kill him," Yesterday says foaming.

"He's killing himself with his ways," Butch replies.

"Man, I got a cool ass celly, Cuzzo. The old dude gave me the bottom bunk and everything," Blue Eyes says.

"My celly is cool, too," Butch says.

"Fuck my celly. I'm not used to having no fucking celly. Watch ya back with these dudes. Ya can't trust them. Oh, here," Yesterday said as he looks down the tier to see if anyone is looking before pulling a knife from his waist. He hands it to Butch. Butch and Blue Eyes just stare at the knife. "Man, put it in your [4]dip or under your mattress,"

"You work fast," Butch says with a mixture of shock and regret.

"I don't be playing. Look, you need to find a hiding spot to keep it. Under your mattress isn't going to work, but sleep with it tonight until you get a good feel of your celly," Yesterday warns.

"I need me one, Cuzzo," Blue Eyes says.

"Give me a minute. I just got two. I told him I would get him one. I got you. Give me a minute to check this spot out and make some shanks," Yesterday says.

_____

[4] *Note: "Put it in your Dip" means to hide a knife under your shirt but in the waist of your pants. It's usually held in place by your belt, tight fitting garments or by a string.*

"Where is Sherman?" Butch asks.

"He went on a visit, Cuzzo" Blue Eyes shares.

"Damn. I'ma see if he can hook me up with some chics. He's one of those quiet smooth dudes. I heard about him on The Hill. The word was that Slim was killing dudes left and right, and making a killing selling crack. Right now, he's probably feeling us out to make sure he can trust us, but Sherm is a gangster," Yesterday says.

They see Sherman walking onto the tier.

"Hey, Sherman. Wussup, Cuzzo?" Blue Eyes shouts.

Sherman stops and looks at them. Blue Eyes starts walking toward him. Butch runs in his cell to stash his knife. Yesterday follows behind Blue Eyes. Sherman sees his cell buddy is in the cell so he keeps walking toward Blue Eyes and Yesterday. He shakes Blue Eyes' extended hand. Then he shakes Yesterday's hand as Butch comes walking down the tier.

"How was your visit, Cuzzo?" Blue Eyes asks.

Sherman looked quizzically at him, "It was cool. Why? Wussup?"

"No reason, Cuzzo" Blue Eyes replies.

"So, can you hook me up with a woman?" Yesterday asked with excitement.

"Naw. I don't have it like that," Sherman says dryly.

The electric cell doors open, close, then open back up. "Chow time," Sergeant Jackson screams from behind the guard station.

"I'm hungry as shit. Ya going?" Yesterday says as he rubs his stomach.

"Yessir. I'm hungry as hell, Cuzzo," Blue Eyes says.

"Yea," Butch responds.

Veins, BH Bandit, Mitch, and Big Bob come walking down the tier from the shower area.

"Naw, I'll holla at ya later, " Sherman says.

"Blue Eyes," Big Bob shouts.

Blue Eyes sees Big Bob waving him over to him.

"Hold up ya'll. I'ma walk with ya,' Blue Eyes says to his friends. Then he walks down to Big Bob and his friends who are standing in front of Blue Eyes' cell. "Wussup, Cuzzo?" Blue Eyes asks Big Bob. Veins and BH Bandit smile as they nod their heads at him. "Wussup, Men," he says.

"You got it, Blue Eyes," Veins says smiling.

"You ok?" Big Bob says as he nods his head toward Yesterday and the others. They are looking toward Blue Eyes.

"Yea. Why you ask me that, Cuzzo?"
Blue Eyes asks. He notices that Veins
has puffy dope fiend hands covered with
blotches. A few blotches are on his neck
from shooting heroin into the veins in his
neck. There are no visible veins on his
hand. He is the only one with a long
sleeve shirt on to hide his arms.

"Do you know those dudes?" Big Bob
questions with concern.

"Yea. We rode over here together,
Cuzzo," Blue Eyes says.

"I'm just making sure you're ok. You
can't befriend any and everybody.
Dudes that seem cool ain't always cool.
I'm just trying to look out for my new
celly. Are you going to chow?" Big Bob
says.

"Yea," Blue Eyes replies.

"Can you bring me back some bread?"
Big Bob asks.

"Yea. I guess. I got'cha, Cuzzo," Blue
Eyes says.

Big Bob pulls out some clear plastic from his pocket and hands it to Blue Eyes. "Look, you are going to have to sneak it out. We aren't allowed to bring food out. Can you do that for me, Celly?" Big Bob asks.

Blue Eyes hunches his shoulder, "I don't see why not, Cuzzo, " Blue Eyes replies.

Big Bob pats him on his shoulder, "Thanks. You're looking out for me already. That's what celly's are suppose to do," Big Bob says smiling.

Blue Eyes smile and walks back toward his friends. Other prisoners start appearing from the shower area on their way down the tier to chow.

Sherman salutes his new buddies before they walk off the tier. Sherman walks into his cell. His bed roll is on his bare mattress on the top bunk. Jessie immediately stands from lying on the bottom bunk. His hands are down at his waist but Sherman can tell the super hero built old man is ready to go to war with him.

"Wussup? How can I help you?" Jessie says as he loosens his neck by leaning his head side to side.

Sherman stands at a respectful distance, but ready to go to war if need be. "I'm your new celly," Sherman says calmly, but firmly. His eyes never looking away from Jessie's eyes.

"I don't live with cowards, faggots or snitches. So, if you are anyone of those, I suggest you move your shit out now," Jessie threatens.

"I guess we won't have a problem unless you want one," Sherman says.

Jessie smirks. "We good then," Jessie says as he lays back down on his bed. Sherman goes and starts making up his bed.

Chapter 11

Yesterday, Butch, and Blue Eyes are walking up the compound. Butch is observing everything and everyone. Goosebumps run up his body. He can sense danger around him. There are close to one hundred men in front of them. Some of the men are walking toward the kitchen. The others are standing around on the sidewalk and behind them are men pouring out of Cell Block Two. The men lingering around make Butch and Blue Eyes more uncomfortable as they lock eyes with them. Both men immediately look away from each set of eyes that look into theirs. The starers are distant yet menacing. Yesterday is too busy talking to them that he doesn't even notice the staring eyes all around them.

Butch notices the three cell blocks on the other side of the compound. The grassy area that separates both groups of cell blocks is half the length and width of a football field. He recognizes that each of those cell blocks have the number one, three or five painted on the door. Butch looks around at the cell block closest to him and sees the number four painted on the door. He notes that his side is even number cell blocks and the other side of the compound are the odd numbered cell blocks.

Butch sees Skip along with Psycho, Razor and Bear walk up to eight more Aryan Brothers that are waiting for them on the walkway. He assumes they are standing in front of cell block six. Butch notices some different prisoners engaged in what he believes to be drug transactions. Suga and Nancy are giggling with four other homosexuals on the side of the walkway near the kitchen entrance doors. The other homosexuals are staring at them with curiosity and sexual interest. He notices a man that he believes is high on heroin near the open door way of the kitchen. The man is bent half over and nodding. Then Big Moe, John, Wayne and Kenny walk passed them. The four men are scanning the faces of each man they passes. Butch lowers his eyes when he looks into John's menacing eyes. He waits a minute to look back *and sees John and his crew heading into Cell Block Two. He refocuses on what's in front of him. He passes a building before the kitchen that has the number seven painted on the door. He thought to himself that is confusing.*

Chapter 12

Sherman is seated at the bottom end of his bunk with his feet dangling in between his cell buddy's bed and toilet/sink combo near the door. He is eating a honey bun. At the top end of the bunk are pictures of Ella and Loretta pasted to the side of the wall near his pillow. Jessie is asleep with his boots on. His body is facing the wall.

"Hey, Sherman," John says respectfully from the doorway. Big Moe, Wayne and Kenny are standing behind him. Sherman's heart immediately starts pounding. Jessie awakes and looks over to the doorway. "I'm sorry, Champ for waking you. Sherman, I need to holla at you," John says demandingly. Sherman jumps down off of the bed as the others step back from the doorway. Sherman walks out into the hallway.

"Wussup, Sherm," Big Moe says with a mixture of happiness and regret. John and the other men are just staring at Sherman. John violates what is considered a respectable distance as he steps closer to Sherman.

"Sherman, you have to get off of the compound ASAP," John says.

Anger races through Sherman, "I'm not going nowhere," Sherman responds in the calmest voice his anger would allow.

Big Moe steps in between John and Sherman as Wayne and Kenny slyly ease their shanks out from their waist. Wayne and Kenny step closer to Sherman.

"Hold on! It ain't going down like that. Ya family. We're family. It has to be a better way to do this," Big Moe pleads as he extends his arms to hold Kenny and Wayne back.

Jessie's head is tilted upward as he stares at the open cell door. He can hear every word. However, he can only see the side of Kenny's body and Sherman's right shoulder. He sees Kenny's shank gripped in his hand but hidden behind his leg.

"Moe, ain't no other way. Shit happened that can't be undone," John snaps back with a hint of regret.

"John, all you had to do was tell me that was your brother and that shit wouldn't have made it that far. Why you didn't just tell me?" Sherman asks in a calmer tone.

"Sherman, what's done is done. You did what you did and I did what I did. So, here we are. Take this opportunity and check-in so I won't have to kill you, Sherman," John says.

"I'm not checking in and I'm not beefing. So, if you still want to get it on, lets do it," Sherman says as he stands ready to fight the men and their knives.

Big Moe turns and pushes his companions further back as John snatches his shank from his waist. Kenny and Wayne are eagerly waiting. "Hold the fuck up! The first one of ya that moves, I'ma knock you the fuck out," Big Moe barks at all of them. He looks to John but continues to scan the movement of each man.

"Why the fuck are ya beefing over a misunderstanding? Ok, your brother got killed. I understand your pain. John, I never knew you didn't tell him who Tim was. But are you hearing Sherman? He said he ain't beefing with you over what you did to him. So, why can't ya squash this shit," Big Moe says as he looks from one to the other.

"Would you let that shit go?" John asks.

"John, ain't shit that can happen right now will bring your brother back. He said he forgave you for what you did. Come on, John. I know ya miss each other. We been through too much together to start killing each other. That's what's wrong with black folks now. We don't love each other," Big Moe says.

John, Sherman, and Kenny start smiling but their smile vanishes as quickly as their smiles appeared. Wayne is laughing his ass off.

"John! Time for you and the rest of those fuck ups to get the hell off of my tier," Sergeant Jackson shouts from the gate.

"Aight, Jackson," John says without taking his eyes off of Sherman. "Let me think about this, Sherman. But for now, stay the fuck out of my way. Don't approach me. Don't try to talk to me. Don't send me messages," John says as he backs up slowly, puts his shank away, and walks toward the gate. Kenny and Wayne follow but walk backwards until they are off the tier.

Moe smiles and extends his hand to Sherman. Sherman smiles back and extends his hand. Moe dismisses his hand and wraps him in a huge and loving bear hug. He almost lifts Sherman off of his feet but Sherman presses all of his weight downward. "Man, I missed you, Sherman! I was hurt they sent me back here and ya on The Hill. Look we're going to make it through this. I'ma make sure this shit gets squashed. You know that fool loves you like a brother. He just crazy as hell but I'ma make sure it's done. You need anything?" Big Moe asks sincerely as he releases him.

"Naw. I'm good," Sherman replied.

Big Moe looks back toward the gate. John and the others are waiting for Sergeant Jackson to open the gate. Sergeant Jackson is walking over to the controls. Big Moe then lifts his shirt to reveal two shanks in his waist. "You need a shank," Big Moe says.

"Naw. I stay strapped," Sherman says smiling.

Big Moe starts laughing, "Sheed. You know I know that. Let me know if you need anything. I'm in Cell Block Three, A-23 Upper," Big Moe says.

"Moe! Come on, Man," John shouts.

"Get your ass off my tier or you're going to the hole! Move it, jail bird," Sergeant Jackson shouts.

They shake hands. "I love you, Sherm," Big Moe says as he is walking away. But then he turns to Sherman as

Sherman is heading back in the cell, "Sherm," Big Moe says. Sherman stops and looks at him. "You know these weren't for you. These are for these new suckers that haven't figured out how to control their emotions and [5]do their bits", Big Moe says as he pats the shanks under his shirt. Then he walks off.

Sherman watches them exit the building. Then he walks into the cell and collapses into a seizure. Jessie sits up from playing sleep. He looks at Sherman having his attack. "You bitch ass nigga. I told you I don't live with cowards," he shouts as he gets out of bed. He grabs Sherman by his legs and drags him onto the tier and leaves him there shaking.

Yesterday, Blue Eyes, and Butch along with other prisoners are walking into the building from the kitchen. They are standing in the doorway waiting for Sergeant Jackson to open the first gate to the cellblock. Yesterday spots

---

[5] *Note: "Bit" mean doing prison time or serving a prison sentence. Example: I'm doing a five year bit.*

Sherman's body on the ground convulsing.

"Open this motherfucking gate! Open this motherfucking gate!" Yesterday screams at Sergeant Jackson. Jackson removes his hand from the lever to open the door and puts his hands on his waist.

"Fuck you. What you going to do if I don't," Sergeant Jackson snaps.

"If my man dies, me and you are going to have some problems," Yesterday shouts with a mixture of panic and anger. Sergeant Jackson looks around. He spots Sherman laid out on the floor flopping around.

"Ya are staying right there!," Sergeant Jackson barks. Then he turns toward the tiers and screams at the few men on the tiers, "Lock down! Lock down! Everybody in their cells...Now," he shouts as he whips out his walkie-talkie. "Man, down on A Lower in Cell Block Two! Send back up!" Sergeant Jackson yells into his walkie talkie as he approaches the gate near Sherman.

"Sarge, open the gate! Let me in,
"Yesterday screams.

Sergeant Jackson points toward
them without looking back at him.
"You're staying right there! All of you! So
shut the hell up! Men on upper B, Lower
B and Upper A! Get your asses in your
cell now!

Chapter 13

Larry is blocking Skip's entrance into the cell. He's standing there with a wife-beater on and his arms folded across his chest.

"Excuse me," Skip calmly says.

"I see you have some new playmates. I can't live like this. Some changes are going to have to be made," he threatens.

Psycho, Bear and Razor walk up behind Skip. "Do we have a problem, Bro," Psycho says staring daringly into Larry's eyes as Razor visibly spits two razor blades from opposite sides of his cheeks and holds them in-between both index fingers of his hands. Bear rotates his neck and the sounds of his bones crackle. " We can take care of that right now," Psycho continues.

Larry chuckles as he makes his chest muscles jump. "We might just have one," he replies loudly, [6]"So all you Crackers want to bring me a move, huh?" he shouts.

"Hold up. Hold up. Hold up," Skip barks. "Ain't nobody bringing you no move, Man. You can't keep trying to put the press on me. If I got a problem with you, you and I are going to handle that one on one. I don't need no gang. I'ma man. I might be a white boy or cracker as you say, but I am all man. We bleed the same. Ain't nothing you can do to me that I can't do to you," Skip warns as twenty correctional officers stampede down the tier. Seven officers including Sergeant Jackson stop and surround the men as the other officers either run through the showers to the upper level or check the cells on the bottom tier.

"Are you bastards hard of hearing or do we have a fucking problem?" Sergeant Jackson snaps.

---

[6] "Bring me a move" means to try and hurt someone. Example: "You Crackers want to bring me a move..."Put the press on me" means to intimidate, to rob, to extort. Example: ya trying to put the press on me?

Razor yawns as he covers his mouth, he drops the razors onto his tongue. Nobody else moves. Then Sergeant Jackson locks eyes with Larry.

"Do we have a problem?" Sergeant Jackson demands.

Larry smiles and backs up, "No, Sir," he says. Then Psycho steps backwards and all of his crew except Skip follow suit. Skip walks into the cell.

"I'll be down as soon as the doors pop," Psycho says to Skip. Skip nods his approval as he jumps on his bunk.

Chapter 14

Susan swiftly walks into the examining room at the prison's medical unit. Sherman is laying on the examining table. He looks up as she leans over him with sadness in her eyes. "Are you ok, baby," she asks as she runs her finger on the side of his temple.

"Are you going to feel me up with the door open?" he says. He looks drained but his voice is strong. She immediately goes and shuts the door and rushes back to his side.

"What happened?" she says as she massages his temple.

"I had a seizure," he says as he sits up.

"Seizure? I've never known you to have those," she says with a startled look.

"They started after I got stabbed," he replied.

"What has the doctor said? Are you suppose to be taking medication for it?" she says as she caresses his shoulder.

"Naw. I'm good. I haven't even seen this doctor yet, but the doctor on The Hill said it should stop," he said.

"Do you want me to call Ella and tell John?" she asks.

"What? Tell John?" he responds.

"Yea. He's over here now. I saw him after I saw you and told him what cell block you were in. I'm surprised he hasn't been to see you," she says.

Sherman sighs.

"What's wrong?" she says.

"Nothing. Look, don't tell nobody shit. I'm good. How did you know I was over here?" he says. She puts her hand on her hip and smirks.

"Really? Really? Sherman. Once I heard them calling a code in your block, I hauled tail down there. They had moved you up here by the time I got there so I re-routed. You know I'ma make sure you're alright," She says as she steps in between his legs and kisses him on his forehead then lips.

He pulls away. "Susan, the doctor hasn't even been in to see me yet. Chill out," he warns.

"Sherman, I haven't been touched in one whole year. I was so pissed when they sent me over here. You know I would have found my way into that hole to take care of you and myself," she says laughing. He nudges her from in between his legs.

"So, you're assigned to the visiting room?" he asks.

"I'm a floater," she replies.

"Can you get to my unit any time you want?" Sherman questions.

"That depends on where I am. Most of the time I can move around or request where I want to go, but during my lunch break, I can run around. Why?" she asks.

"I need a knife," he says staring into her eyes.

"Sherman. Come on. Don't start acting up over here. You know I'm looking out for you so no more drugs, no more shanks, and no more violence. Come on. We're trying to make parole this time, right?" she says, forcing a smile.

"I need a knife," he says seriously.

"No," she says pouting.

He stands and wraps his arms around her and kisses her on her lips. As soon as she starts kissing him back, he pulls away. "Don't ever tell me no again. I need a Butcher's knife. Not a shank. I want a Butcher's knife or one of those hunting knives with the ridged edges," he says before sitting back down on the examining table.

She pouts, folds her arms and taps her foot and sighs. Then she glances to the door and back at him. " I guess I can get you a knife out of the kitchen," she says as he shakes his head.

"No. They count those knives. They'll keep us locked down until they find it. I need one from the streets. I need it tomorrow," he declares.

"How am I suppose to get that in here?" she asks.

"Susan, now we know you can get whatever you want in here," he smiles.

She smiles back. "I guess, but I can't seem to get you out of here," she says. He reaches out and caresses her hand.

"I'm getting out. I go see the parole board again in three months," he says.

"Then why do you need that? I don't get you, Sherman. You have two women who love you and a beautiful daughter but you still act like the rest of these guys. This isn't The Hill, Sherman. These guys don't play," she warns him.

"Susan, I'm new here. You know these dudes are going to try me. They don't care shit about me going up for parole. If anything, that'll give them more reason to come at me. I wanna protect me. You want me to die when I am so close to coming home?" he says.

She groans like a little girl. "No-ooo".

"Well, I need that knife ASAP. I would appreciate it if you could bring me some syringes too," he says.

"What's that for?! You getting high now?" She snaps angrily.

"Don't play with me," he says with a menacing stare. His expression then softens and turns into a smile, "Oh, by the way, Congratulations. I see you made Sergeant! Yay yea," he says jokingly. She starts giggling.

"Wow. I didn't think you would notice. You're so self-centered," she says laughing.

"Ahhhhhh. That hurts," he replies. Then they both look at the door when the door knob turns. The nurse steps into the room.

"Nurse, I'm going to step out. If you need me, I'll be outside the door. I'll escort him back to his block when you're done," Susan says as she leaves the room.

Chapter 15

Psycho walks past the few men standing around on the tier and stops at the guard's gate. Sergeant Jackson is seated at his desk and writing in the log book. He looks up and sees Psycho's sinister stare turn into a smile.

"Sergeant, can I talk to you for a second?" he says.

Sergeant Jackson struts over to the gate, "What can I do for you, Convict"?

Psycho's eyes squinted with irritation that he quickly fought off. "I am hoping you would honor a request and move Donavon out of the cell he's in and put him in the cell with Holloway?"

"Why? Is Skip Donavon having problems with his cell buddy?" Sergeant Jackson asks.

"No, Sir. He just needs to be in the cell with his own kind," Psycho responds.

"There is no segregation here outside of PC, Convict. If he's having an issue with his cell buddy, I'll put him in protective custody and you don't have to worry about anyone getting to him. How's that?" Sergeant Jackson says sarcastically.

"He's not having a problem. I appreciate your time, Sir," Psycho says through clenched teeth before walking angrily onto the tier. Some of the men on the tier become tense or watch him with aggression as he stomps past them.

Chapter 16

Black Smoke, Yesterday, Marc and Dre are standing on the bottom steps next to the showers. The steps lead to the upper level. Yesterday is standing a step above them with his arms folded across his chest. He's watching all movement. Right now, the only movement is Black Smoke licking his lips and rubbing his hands as he talks to Marc and Dre. He is standing on the floor in front of the bottom of the steps. Marc is leaning on the lower end of the railing and Dre is seated on the steps but slanted between Yesterday and Marc.

"Yea. So the crackers got all the dope in the prison. You know what I'm saying? You know they running it because they got the guards bringing it in. You know what I am saying? Anyway, Psycho usually makes the new dude or the lower ranking Aryan stash the shit in his cell or somewhere where he can get to it. You know what I am saying? So that means Skip, the new white dude that came down with you. You know what I

am saying? He will be stashing the shit.
You listening, Yesterday? You know
what I am saying?" Black Smoke says
as he licks his lips and rubs his hands.

"Yea. I hear you," Yesterday replies.

"So that Skip cracker is soft. You know
what I'm saying? You can look at him
and tell that. You know what I am
saying? I heard he got an accidental
body or he killed his mother or
something. You know what I am saying?
Anyway, he sleeps on the lower tier. You
know what I'm saying? Now Razor
keeps all of the shanks and Bear is
more the muscle. So if we can catch
Skip in the cell by himself, it's on. You
know what I'm saying?" Black Smoke
says excitedly as he continues to lick his
lips and rub his hands.

"Smoke, the dude Skip is in the cell with
a brother. They're not going to stash that
shit in there with him," Marc says.

"Yup. They're not going to do that," Dre
says.

"Look, they're going to either get him and Bear in the same cell or Psycho is going to move out of his cell with Razor and into the cell with Skip. You know what I'm saying? I'm hoping Bear moves in there with him. Bear's ass stays high or cleaning the compound so we'll still have a chance to catch Skip alone. You know what I'm saying?" Black Smoke says, licking his lips and rubbing his hands.

"So, what's the plan when we get the shit?" Yesterday asks as he watches Jessie come into the shower, barefoot, with only a towel wrapped around him.

"I'ma get high," Dre says. Black Smoke sees Yesterday frowning at Dre.

"Man, you know I want us to put it on the compound and get some 'chedda. You know what I'm saying?" Black Smoke replies as he continues to lick his lips and rub his hands.

"So you don't expect no retaliation from those other twenty seven or thirty crazy crackers I seen them sitting with in the kitchen?" Yesterday says sarcastically.

"How they going to know who did it? You know what I'm saying? Plus, fuck them crackers. You know what I'm saying? They can act crazy if they want and it will be a race riot on this compound. You know what I'm saying?" Black Smoke says as he is shaking his head, licking his lips, and rubbing his hands.

They hear the cell doors opening and closing. "Recreation time, Jail Birds! You have two minutes to get out of the Block," Sergeant Jackson shouts.

Dre' pops up. "I'm going in the yard. Ya going?" Dre asks.

"You going, Yesterday?" Black Smoke asks as he licks his lips and rubs his hands.

"Naw. I'm tired. I'ma lay back while ya do ya thing," Yesterday replies.

"Damn. I wanna introduce you to more of my team. You know what I'm saying?" Black Smoke says, nodding his head, licking his lips, and rubbing his hands.

"Where are they going? Are they getting out tomorrow? If not, I have plenty of decades to meet them," Yesterday says.

"True. True," Black Smoke says as he licks his lips and rubs his hands. "Are ya strapped?" Black Smoke asks his other two comrades as he licked his lips and rubbed his hands.

They nod their heads that they are. They shake Yesterday's hand before walking down the tier. He steps off the steps.

From his peripheral vision he sees Jessie in the shower with his back to him and his head under the shower head. The man is naked with no shower shoes on. Yesterday pulls off all of his clothes except for his boxers and boots and folds them on the steps. His shank is sticking out of the waistline of his boxers. He snatches the shank free and dashes into the shower. Jessie spins around in defense mode. They circle each other.

"What's your beef, Youngsta," Jessie says confused but ready to fight.

"I'm reducing your mothafuckun sentence. It's time for you to go home to your maker," Yesterday says sinisterly.

"Youngsta, I ain't never do nothing to you. Why you got beef with me," Jessie snaps as they continue to circle each other.

"Fuck dat. Just take it, you got beef," Yesterday snaps.

"Well, fuck it. I'ma make you eat that knife," Jessie says confidently.

Yesterday jerks as if he is going to attack. Jessie backs up but tries to charge him and slips and falls face first onto the shower floor. Yesterday stabs him instantly in the back before jumping on top of him and stabbing him once on the side of his neck and once in the back of his neck. Blood squirts in both directions before mixing with the water and disappearing down the drain. Then he pushed the knife into Jessie's heart from his back. His body begins convulsing. As Yesterday stands, he plunges the blade through the back of the man's scalp. Blood squirts and begins trickling down the blade, across his back and onto the shower floor. Yesterday scans the area. He jumps underneath the shower and rinses the blood off himself and quickly scrubs the shank with Jessie's soap. Then he swiftly grabs his clothes and heads up the steps to his cell.

Chapter 17

There are about two hundred men talking, working out, playing basketball, jogging with headphones on, walking along the wall, or scheming all over the recreation yard. The men segregated themselves by their race.

Butch is nodding his head in agreement as Rocket talks to him, Blue Eyes, and some other older prisoners seated on one of the many picnic tables scattered in different areas of the yard . Rakeys is showing another prisoner a case in his law book that Rakeys believes will overturn the man's life sentence.

Skip is standing a few feet behind a dozen Aryan Brothers. The Aryans are deep in several conversations. Bear and another Aryan seem to be scanning the yard in search of someone. Bear grabs the ends of the wet towel around his neck. He glances back and sees Skip leaning against the wall. Skip is looking nervously around and focuses for brief periods at the ground.

The guy standing next to Bear nudges him. Bear sees Psycho and Razor walking onto the yard among several other prisoners that include Black Smoke, Dre', and Marc.

Psycho and Razor greet Bear after acknowledging the rest of the brotherhood.

"How's everything, Brother?" Psycho questions.

Bear nods toward Skip. Skip is now leaning against the wall. His hands gripped around the back of his head with his eyes closed toward the sun. Psycho walks over to Skip.

"You look like you're about to piss your fucking pants, Brother," Psycho says as he aggressively grips the back of Skip's head with one of his hands. "Open your eyes."

Skip's red eyes open and he stares sadly into Psycho's eyes.

"Are you a homo," Psycho says gripping Skip's head tighter. Then he grips the back of Skip's head with both of his hands. "Do you want to be a fucking homo, Brother?"

Skip shakes his head no as he lowers his eyes.

Psycho snatches his head back up. "Brother? Brother?" Psycho says with a calmer tone.

Skip stares him in his eyes.

"I can feel your fucking knees trembling...Do you remember how easy it was for you to kill that nigger that got you here," Psycho demands.

Skip nods his head that he remembers.

"This isn't no different than that," Psycho says as Bear steps up beside him. He looks Psycho in his eyes and nods his head toward the black man who sat in the visiting room with his wheelchair bound mother with the oxygen tank. The man's black belt is dangling over his left shoulder. He appears to be arguing with two other black men. Psycho nods his head that he sees the man. Then he turns his focus back to Skip as Bear walks back to his position. "These are your options, Brother. You can either go kill that nigger and get your tats or you can die, right here and right now by me, after you drop to your knees and suck my cock. I promise, I'll slit your throat as soon as I cum. Do you want to suck my dick or get your tats? You wanna get your tats, right?"

Skip nods his head in agreement. Psycho gently smacks him on his cheek as he leans on the wall beside him. "See that nigger with his belt hanging over his shoulder? That's your target. You won't have any problems out of the blacks. They know this is coming, but we'll be with you regardless. Take this," Psycho says as he retrieves a shank from his lower back.

Skip's trembling hand takes the knife and holds it behind his leg. Psycho leans against Skip's shaking shoulders. "Do you want something to calm your shakes?" Psycho says.

Skip shakes his head no.

"Now I want you to walk down toward the gate like you're trying to go to the housing unit, but turn back. You causally walk behind the guy. Snatch his head in the opposite direction then you jam this fucking blade in his neck. Hit him twice and let him go. Push the knife in him as far as it can go when you hit him. Then walk back toward the housing unit. Drop the piece in the grass and exit the yard. Go".

Skip walks toward the exit gate to get to the housing unit. He turns and walks within three feet of the man before the man is alarmed. The man spins around in defense mode and throws a punch at Skip. The punch scrapes Skip's chin, but Skip is able to grab a hold of the man's arm and just starts stabbing him. The man swings wildly, but Skip continues to stab him in his upper body until the man drops to one knee. Skip jams the blade in the front of the man's head. He jerks the blade back and forth until it stops at the center of the man's head. Blood squirts from the wound onto Skip's shirt and face. The man's body convulses before death. Skip yanks the knife free as the stunned prisoners stare, those who haven't already started exiting the yard, start walking briskly. Skip starts walking toward the exit as the Aryan's walk toward him spreading out. As soon as Skip drops the knife, another Aryan picks it up, wipes it with a cloth, and tosses it into the Black's area. He heads toward the exit. Another Aryan walks up and rips Skip's shirt off his back right before Bear walks up and wipes all visible blood from his hands, arms, chest, and face. He tosses the towel in the Black's area and walks toward the exit. Psycho tosses Skip a t-shirt.

"Put it on now," Psycho says with urgency. Skip puts it on. Psycho raps his arm around Skip's shoulder. "You're an evil motherfucker! You're going to fucking get your beautiful tear drop! I fucking love it when we can show we killed another nigger. You're such a crazy fucker, we're going to cover your fucking face with tats so these assholes will know you're fucking vicious!" Psycho says with pure excitement.

Guards begin to look around the yard from the exit gate. Too much brisk walking for something not to have happened.

Chapter 18

Blue Eyes is desperately trying to see into the shower area from inside his cell. From time to time, he sees someone from the administration or police department walk past his cell. He hasn't seen them carry the body out yet, but he has seen them carry bags of evidence or what he believes to be evidence down the tier. "Damn two stabbings around the same time. "The white boys don't be faking. They tore holes in that dude in the yard. I wonder who that was that they hit up in the shower. Damn. I hope it wasn't Sherman because they been in and out of his cell. Plus, I didn't see him in the cell when I came in," Blue Eyes says before looking up at Big Bob on his top bunk. Big Bob is smiling at him.

"That violence shit sure excites you, youngstas. Ya crazy," Big Bob exclaims. "Get away from that door before they think you know something," he demands. Blue Eyes looks at him as if he is going to say something but *changes his mind. He goes and sits down on the bottom bunk.*

"I bet you used to get all of the girls with those eyes," Big Bob says jokingly.

"I did my thang. The chicks loved them, but the dudes hated me all my life for them, Cuzzo. These eyes can get the chicks, but they can't keep them, Cuzzo. My girl left me after I got sentenced, Cuzzo," Blue Eyes says with a little sadness in his voice.

Big Bob jumps down and starts pissing in the toilet. Blue Eyes turns his head because he can see the man's penis.

"Big Bob, come on, Cuzzo! I can see your shit. Face the motherfucking toilet, Cuzzo!" Blue Eyes snaps.

Big Bob starts laughing but he turns his penis from view. "No disrespect, Youngsta. We all men, right?" Big Bob coos.

"Yea, I'm a motherfucking man, Cuzzo," Blue Eyes snaps as irritation sets in.

Big Bob shakes his penis as he finishes relieving himself. Then he turns toward Blue Eyes. "Calm down. I already told you I meant no disrespect," Big Bob says with a hint of aggression. Blue Eyes is looking down at his hands and shaking his head. "But you know ain't no young girl going to do no forty to life prison bit with you. You here with us long timers now. Shit. I have ninety-six years. Everybody left me as soon as I got sentenced. So, we all we got, Celly. The sooner you can cross them females out of your mind, the easier it's going to get for you to do your time. Thinking about women you can't catch up with is going to drive you crazy. Trust me, I know. Just focus on making the best life you can make for yourself in here. I'ma teach you everything I know. I got your back.

"I ain't never going to stop thinking about no females, Cuzzo" Blue Eyes mutters.

Chapter 19

Rocket is leaning on the wall of the cell and looking up at Butch. Butch is seated on the top end of his bunk. "Now that was some initiation crap for that white boy that came down here with ya. That asshole he stabbed is, simply put, an asshole. His mother is better off without him. He had that sick woman breaking her back to get down here and she giving him most of her social security money. I heard a few times he convinced her to sneak some pills in for him to sell. So, damn disgraceful. He should have been dead a decade ago when he first got down here. Damn Junky," *Rocket says foaming. He shakes his head with disgust.* " Sorry about the rambling. Anyway, he could have been killed for multiple stupid reasons but if the Aryan's did it and no blacks jumped in, it was an approved hit. You can bet it had something to do with drugs. All those white boys care about is drug money. Now the stabbing might have been a diversion so they could kill whoever they got in the showers,"

Rocket said with a look as if he just solved the crime.

"Why would they need to create a diversion?" Butch asks innocently.

"Because it looked like all of the white boys were in the yard. See, nobody is going to revenge the asshole in the yard but somebody may seek revenge for whoever they killed in the shower. See, these white boys ain't stupid by a long shot nor are they as scary as they look. All those tattoos on their eyebrows and all over their faces are to make you think they're crazy. Now don't get me wrong, a few of them will kill you in a blink of an eye, but most of them are just hiding. They're outnumbered so bad that it keeps them scared. You know a scared dude will kill you quick. Just think. Every time one of these brothers or Latinos get mad, they blame the white man for putting them here, and those Aryans are their targets. Most of them don't have a problem killing you because they're hoping to get to the Feds where there are more of their kind. However, they can't get to the feds for killling a nigga,

you got to kill a guard to get to the feds,"
Rocket informs.

"But the white boy that stabbed the dude
in the yard didn't get caught. So he can't
be trying to go to the feds," Butch
explains.

"You're right. That thing in the yard was
their way of saying, 'We got another
vicious killa on our team and he doesn't
have a problem killing one of you
niggers in front of all you niggers. White
Power!" Rocket says before bursting
into laughter as he holds his right palm
in the air as if he was a Nazi soldier.

Chapter 20

BH Bandit is seated on the top bunk drawing. Yesterday is lying on the bottom bunk with his palms behind his head. He's staring straight up at the bottom of the top bunk. Their cell door goes dark as Sergeant Jackson and seven nightstick carrying officers are standing in the opening door way. Both prisoners look over at the Sergeant.

"Get the fuck on the wall! Get on the wall! Get on the wall!" Sergeant Jackson screams as the officers fill the room behind him. BH Bandit leaps off the bunk and plants his hands on the wall around the small window. Yesterday eases up into a seated position.

"What ya want?" he asks as he slowly starts putting on his shoes. Sergeant Jackson snatches him up and slams the front of his body to the wall. Yesterday tries to resist, but one of the officers presses his nightstick to the back of his neck.

"Get the fuck off of me!" Yesterday shouts.

"You resist, it's your fault if it snaps," Sergeant Jackson says smiling as two other officers cuff both men.

"What we do, Sarge?" BH Bandit questions.

"Shut up," Sergeant Jackson snaps. "Take the old one in the hall. Take this one to the hole," Sergeant Jackson orders as the officer with the nightstick removes his weapon. "I want ya to tear this cell up. Find me a murder weapon," Sergeant Jackson says as two officers escort BH Bandit out of the cell.

"A murder weapon," Yesterday says with confusion. Sergeant Jackson steps up to his face as the officers prepare to walk him out of the cell.

"Remember, I saw you screaming and shouting when Mr. Ford was on the floor," Sergeant Jackson says calmly.

"What in the fuck does that mean? I saw a man in need of medical attention," Yesterday says calmly.

"That means suspect to me, Sir. Get him out of here," Sergeant Jackson says as two of the remaining officers start snatching up their mattresses and the other one checks around the toilet.

Black Smoke and Dre are cell buddies. They are standing at their closed cell door and staring into Yesterday's cell.

"Wussup, Yesterday? You know what I'm saying?" Black Smoke questions as he licks his lips and rubs his hands.

"Nothing," Yesterday replies.

Black Smoke licks his lips and rubs his hands together as he nods his head in agreement and walks away from the cell door. "Be strong, Champ. Don't say nothing. Don't say nothing," Dre' chants.

Sergeant Jackson walks out of the cell. "Grab him, too!" Sergeant Jackson says pointing to Dre's cell.

"Sergeant, I didn't do shit," Dre' pleads.

Butch is back at his cell door as they walk Yesterday and Dre' past. "What happened?" he asks. Yesterday just shakes his head. Butch looks at Rocket, "They just locked my buddy up."

"The plot thickens," Rocket says humorously.

Chapter 21

Skip repositions himself in bed. Larry's eyes pop open from his sleep because of Skip's movement. He sighs and eases his knife out of his pillowcase. Skip's eyes pop open. He sighs and repositions his shank next to his groin. They both lie there all night listening for any movement from the other.

Chapter 22

Sergeant Jackson stands up from behind his desk and takes the ring of keys off of his belt and hands them to the officer that just came on duty. He stretches as the other officer sits down behind the desk. The officer attaches the keys to his belt. Then Sergeant Jackson walks over to the middle of the gate that faces the tiers. "Lights out, Jail birds!" he shouts before walking over to the switchboard and dimming the lights on the tiers.

Big Bob looks over his bunk at the sleeping Blue Eyes, "Celly," he whispers. Blue Eyes doesn't respond. He digs in his boxers and retrieves a shank from his rectum before removing his boxers. He then eases off of the bunk and lays flat on top of Blue Eyes' back. Blue Eyes' eyes pop open with an alarming stare. Big Bob snatches back the man's neck by gripping his forehead. He sticks the point of the shank against Blue Eyes throat. Blue Eyes tries to turn but the weight of the man's body is too much. He continues to try to thrust side to side. Big Bob pierces some of Blue Eyes skin with the shank. "Either it's going to be shit on my dick or blood on my knife," He whispers into his ear as they hear the screams of another man being raped somewhere in the distance.

"Get off me, Cuzzo. Get the fuck off of me," Blue Eyes says through gritted teeth. Big Bob snatches the top of Blue Eyes head further back and places the tip of the shank underneath his Adam's Apple. He can't talk or move.

"Kill yo self. I like my ass dead or alive," he says as he snatches down the teenager's pants and boxers. Water fills Blue Eyes' eyes as Big Bob jerks his penis erect before forcing himself inside him. Blue Eyes grits his teeth as his rectum tears. Big Bob immediately uses his other freehand to snatch the teenager's head further back as Blue Eyes' tries to slam his neck down on the blade. After Big Bob finishes thrusting and relieving himself inside of Blue Eyes, he snatches the shank away from his throat and starts pounding him in the face with his fist. He then jumps up and starts furiously kicking him. Blue Eyes folds himself into the fetal position. Big Bob then stands up with the shank in his hand.

"From now on you keep this cell clean. You piss sitting down. You don't grow no hair on your motherfucking face. You keep your legs shaved and you stay away from my motherfucking knives," he snaps before walking over to the toilet and starts taking a piss. He speaks over his shoulder, " Also, the other chics around here wear some kind of eyeliner. I want you to get you some of that. I like that. You need to get more feminine. I like that, Boo." After he finished pissing, he tugs at Blue Eyes foot. Blue Eyes snatches his foot away and remains in the fetal position. "Look, we need each other. You got life. I have three life sentences, two of them for killing my bitches in my cell. But look, I been locked up for 30 years. Shit that's twelve years longer than you been alive. So, you're going to have to trust my wisdom on this. Don't worry, I'ma let everybody know tomorrow that you're my pussy." He climbs back on his bunk and lies down holding his knife at the ready.

Chapter 23

Sherman kisses Susan passionately as her naked lower body holds him firmly in between her legs and inside of her on the examining table. He climaxes and kisses her down to her navel as he pulls his pants up. He stands. Her hands clammer for him. He holds her hands in his and smiles.

"You know we can't be in here all day," he says.

She rises and wraps her arms and legs around him. "I am so tired of sharing you," she mutters.

"Well, we don't have a choice. I'm afraid the institution wouldn't allow you to openly fuck me in the hospital," he says laughing.

"I never fuck you. We always make love. You don't consider this making love to me? Is this just a fuck for you?" she pouts.

He flattens her eyebrows with his thumbs. "You are so dramatic," he replies.

"Plus, I wasn't talking about sharing you with this place. I'm tired of sharing you with Ella," she confides.

He frowns, pulls away from her and walks toward the door. She runs and leans her back on the door. She holds him back with her fingers. "Why are you mad?" she whispers.

"I don't want to argue with you. I just want to go back to my block," he says staring in her eyes.

Her eyes water. "Sherman, you know you can't go back down there until they finish their investigation," she says tearfully. "Sherman, I'm tired of taking all of the risk and all I get is fucked. I deserve your heart. I deserve the man. I deserve you, Sherman. Why do I have to settle for being fucked? Tell me, Sherman. Tell me you don't love me and I will leave you alone. I swear I will walk away. You won't have any problems out of me. I just need to hear what's on your heart," she says crying and pointing to his heart.

He pulls her into his arms and kisses the top of her head. "You know I love you," he says. She wraps her arms tighter around him, leans her head on his chest and smiles.

Chapter 24

Big Moe is looking down from his top bunk at John. John is stooped in between the toilet and the wall near the cell door. He keeps peeping out the cell and down the tier as he sharpens a piece of seven inch metal into a shank by filing it against the bottom edge of the metal door frame. "I'ma kill Sherman during breakfast," John confesses.

"Come on, John! Ya family. You see he's not beefing. He was more apologetic because how all of this went down," Moe pleads.

"Sherman is sneaky," John says before pausing and staring into Moe's eyes. "Would you forgive me for trying to kill you?"

"It's hard to say," Moe says.

"Right," John says before peeping down the tier then continuing to sharpen his weapon.

"Well, look at it this way, you know he can get as much drugs as he wants in here. He got the white chic to get it in and the connect to get it from. Just think. Remember the money we were making down Occoquan? And then you tell me ya had the crack game on lockdown on The Hill. Think about the money we could be making off of heroin in here! I wanna make some money. I know you wanna stack your money. Shit. Sherman is our only way. These white boys ain't going to put us on and that shit they selling is garbage. Imagine if we put that good shit on the compound. Uh? Yea. Money money money monnnnnnney. Fuck beefing. You can beef with whomever you want after I stack me a nest egg big enough to land a helicopter in this motherfucker to take me on a fifty year vacation," Big Moe said as they both laughed.

Chapter 25

5:30am. Sherman walks into his dark cell. Rakeys pops up into a seated position on the bottom bunk. Sherman immediately goes into a defense stance after being startled. "Who the fuck is that?" Sherman barks.

Rakeys leaps up with a knife gripped in his hand. He recognizes Sherman from the dim light on the opposite side of the bars. "Sherman," Rakeys says joyfully.

"Rakeys," Sherman replies with equal joy in his voice. They both burst into laughter. "Man, I was getting ready to beat that ass," Sherman barks playfully.

"I know you caught a glimpse of this blade sparkling beautifully underneath the gangster that burns inside of me. I was going to give you to your God, Champ," Rakeys barks as he twist the shank in his hand under the light that streams into the cell. They laugh as they shake hands.

Then Sherman points to the blade before Rakeys hides it under his cover. "How did you get that so damn fast?" Sherman says in total surprise.

"I grabbed it from under the dirt near the entrance on my way in the building. Ain't no way I'm moving into a dead man cell empty handed. Damn, Sherm. Who would have known?" he says shaking his head. "Where in the fuck you coming from? Did you smash your celly in the shower?" Rakeys questions.

"Naw. I had a seizure and that bitch ass nigga dragged me onto the tier. I guess he had other enemies," Sherman replied.

"Or you have some cool friends," Rakeys replies.

"Naw. A few of these dudes are cool but we ain't like that. So, they smashed him in the shower, huh," Sherman says.

"Yea. They been getting busy in this joint. Dragged your ass on the tier, your cell buddy gets smashed in the shower, and some dude got raped all night long," Rakeys replies.

"Really?" Sherman says.

"Gentlemen, chow time!!!!" Corporal Dickens flickers the switch that controls the cell doors. The doors shake loudly. "You have five minutes," he shakes the doors again before leaving them open. Most of the prisoners, whether half awake or not, look both ways on the tier before walking out of the cell. Big Bob is the first man to step on the tier followed by Skip and Mitch. Mitch lives two cells away from the shower. Big Bob waves his hand at Mitch. Mitch immediately starts smiling and pumping his fist proudly in the air. As he heads toward Big Bob, Psycho, Razor, and Bear whom are leading the pack of men walking from the shower area on to the tier.

"Did you hear my new bitch scream last night?" Mitch screeches as he shakes Big Bob's hand. "I love me a screamer," Mitch brags as Big Bob nods his head toward his cell and smiles. Mitch goes and looks into the cell. He sees Blue

Eyes in the fetal position on the top bunk.

"Let her sleep. She's tired. She's not a screamer but she's a fighter. I beat that bitch ass and put her on the top bunk last night," Big Bob says boisterously.

"Was it good?" Mitch asks.

"What do you think? She has the prettiest blue eyes. That shit alone made me nut," Big Bob brags proudly as they head down the tier as the Aryans shake hands with Skip. The Aryans passes Butch stepping out of his cell. He walks to Blue Eyes' cell and playfully knocks on the bars.

"You going to breakfast. I know your ass is hungry," he playfully shouts to Blue Eyes as Rocket strolls up and looks into the cell. "Blue Eyes! Come on, Man," Butch blurts. Rocket calmly places one hand on Butch's shoulder as he nudges him away from the cell.

"Come on. He's not coming," Rocket says sympathetically.

"Blue! Come on, Man. Aye, Cuzzo!"
Butch shouts still playfully. Rocket pats
Butch on the shoulder.

"I need to talk to you about something.
It's important, Butch," Rocket says. As
they head down the tier, Butch shakes
his head and keeps looking back at Blue
Eyes' cell. Butch then steps into
Sherman's doorway and looks
suspiciously past the back of Sherman
into the eyes of Rakeys. Rakeys
immediately grabs his shank. Sherman
tenses before spinning around with his
hands in a fist. "Wussup, Butch," he
says smiling as he blocks Rakeys from
charging Butch and Rocket.

"Yea. You ok?" Butch asks without
dropping his sinister stares from
Rakey's.

"Yea. This is my main man, Rakeys.
Rakeys meet Butch," Sherman says.

Both of the other men relax.
"Wussup? Sherman, Blue Eyes is going
through something. You may want to
holler at him after breakfast," Butch
suggests.

"Hmm. I'll holla at him now. I'm not going to chow," Sherman says.

Butch nods his head. He and Rocket walk off the tier.

"Sherman, that dude Blue Eyes may have been the one screaming last night," Rakeys says convincingly.

"Damn," Sherman says as he walks out of the cell and down to Blue Eyes' cell. Rakeys grabs his knife and strolls down the tier behind him. Sherman stops in Blue Eyes' door way. Blue Eyes is still in the fetal position. "Hey, Blue, you aight?" he asks. Blue Eyes never responds. Then he starts whimpering. Rakeys shakes his head in disappointment. "Shawty, this doesn't make you less than a man. Don't focus on what happened. Don't let it drown you. Shawty, you have to stand like a man. You have to prove to yourself that you are that same Blue Eyes young gangsta from the street. I know you don't want to hear this, but you have to prove this to yourself that you're still him. Can't nobody else handle this but you," Sherman says like a caring parent.

"How is she?" Suga says as he and Nancy walk up to the cell from the back of the tier. Both Sherman and Rakeys glare at them as they step on the tier to face them.

"Bitch, ain't no shes in here! You see a she in here? Huh," Sherman says as he approaches Suga. Suga and Nancy slowly step backwards. Suga holds up his palms.

"I don't want any problems. I just-I just heard what happened. I'm sorry. I'm really sorry. I don't want any problems. I just want to go to breakfast," Suga pleads.

Rakeys taps Sherman on the side. "This isn't your fight. This isn't your fight. Shawty has to stand on his own toes before you can stand with him. You know the rules. This isn't your fight," Rakeys reminds him. Then Sherman nods his head and they stand to the side as the two homosexuals ease their way past them and briskly walk down the tier.

Sherman walks back to the doorway. "Blue Eyes! Blue Eyes! Did you hear that shit! That motherfucker called you she! You have to straighten this shit! You can't lay up there feeling sorry for your motherfucking self. Get the fuck up and straighten that shit. Do you fucking hear me? That faggot called you a fucking she. Get your shit together or they all will be fucking you! Before I let that happen, I will check your motherfucking ass in PC," Sherman says fuming and jabbing his finger in the air and through the bars as the cell doors close.

Chapter 26

An hour later, Yesterday and Dre' walk onto the empty tier. Yesterday stops at Sherman's cell as Dre' continues through the back shower area to get to the second floor.

"Sherman," Yesterday says leaning on the bars.

Sherman is leaning on the wall and talking to Rakeys who is seated on the top bunk. He looks at him before walking over to the bars. "How was the food?" Sherman asks with a smirk.

"The food?" Yesterday looks bewildered.

"You didn't go to breakfast?" Sherman says.

"Naw. You good? I just wanted to check on you," he genuinely asks.

"I'm good," Sherman says as he sticks his hand out of the bars to shake Yesterday's hand.

"Aight," Yesterday says before walking down to Blue Eyes' cell. Blue Eyes is in extreme pain. He grimaces as he struggles to pull his sheet off of the bed and he winces with every slow step he takes toward the toilet while holding his stomach. "What's wrong with you, Blue?" Yesterday asks with concern.

Blue Eyes is startled. He drops his eyes to the floor as soon as he connects eyes with Yesterday. He makes it to the toilet and grips the sink as the pain rips through him.

Yesterday notices dry blood and dry shit on his legs. "Fuck naw. Shawty, your celly raped you," Yesterday demands. Blue Eyes glances up at him before lowering his eyes again. "Fuck. Fuck. Fuck. Shawty, how you wasn't on point," Yesterday pleads. He looks down the tier and sees Big Bob, BH Bandit, Mitch and Veins walking onto the tier as the cell doors open. He glares at the men. "Blue, I'ma handle that for you, Youngsta," he says before briskly walking down the hall. He nearly knocks Mitch's, young and half naked, cell buddy down as the man exits his cell.

The half naked man is wrapped in a sheet and carrying his shower gear. Yesterday doesn't even notice that the man is in the same pain as Blue Eyes. Yesterday moves around the man and runs through the showers to the upper level. He runs into his cell and as he grabs his shank from its hiding place, Black Smoke appears in the door way. He spins around in attack mode until he recognizes him.

"Wussup? What you about to get into? You know what I'm saying?" Black Smoke asks curiously as he licks his lips and rubs his hands.

"My little man's cell buddy raped him. I'ma punish that bitch," he says through clinched teeth.

Black Smoke blocks his path and grabs Yesterday by his shoulders. "You know that dude has to make the first move. You know what I am saying? You're not helping him if you kill the dude for him. You know what I'm saying? You know these dudes in here will never respect him unless he handles his own beef. Once he initiates it, I'll roll with you. But you have to let him decide if he's going to be a man. You know what I am saying?" he tells him as he licks his lips and rubs his hands.

Yesterday understands but he shakes his head in regret and pity.

"Lock down! Lock down! Lock down...Now!," shouts four guards. Prisoners are swiftly moving into their cells. Yesterday instantly places his shank in the waist of his lower back. He turns to the door as Black Smoke peeps out before stepping onto the tier.

BH Bandit walks in between them to get in the cell, " Some young hoe hung herself in the shower," BH Bandit says disappointedly because now they have to be locked in their cells.

Yesterday snatches him up by his collar and pins him on the wall. BH Bandit is frozen in fear. Black Smoke grabs his wrist before he could pull the shank he just tucked away. "Yesterday, come on. You can't. You know what I am saying? Let it go. Remember what I said. You can't beat this case. The guards are already on the tier. You know what I'm saying?" Black Smoke says before licking his lips.

They see the rage diminish in Yesterday's eyes as he releases the man.

"What the fuck is wrong with you?" BH Bandit barks.

"Get the fuck-," Yesterday was saying before Black Smoke interrupts.

"Bandit, let him be. He's going through something. You know what I'm saying?" Black Smoke says licking his lips and rubbing his hands as two gigantic guards block them.

"Where do you sleep?" Officer Crush demands.

"I sleep over there. You know what I'm saying?" Black Smoke says as he licks his lips and points across the tier to his cell before rubbing his hands.

"Then I suggest you get there, Sir," Officer Crush says threateningly.

Black Smoke nods his head and walks to his cell as BH Bandit jumps up on his top bunk.

Chapter 27

Susan's voice can be heard passing out mail on the tier. Butch is standing at the bars inside his cell and peering down the tier. He can't see her. Rocket is seated on his bed with his feet on the floor.

"Butch, you have been pretty quiet since we been in the cell. You ok?" Rocket says but Butch doesn't respond. He keeps looking out of the cell door. Then Susan stops in front of the door. She has a stack of mail in her hand. Butch tries to hide his excitement but his eyes are gleaming. She tells him to step aside. His disappointment is visible. His head drops and his shoulder slouch. She counts him and Rocket before walking off to the next cell.

Butch looks out the bars again with desperation but hope until Susan completely leaves his view. Sadness consumes him. He taps his finger against the bar as he continues to peer down the tier.

"I know the feeling. I haven't received a piece of mail in twenty two years. People move on with their lives, Butch. I'm sure somebody will write you," Rocket says as he stands.

Butch spins around and positions himself in a defense stance. Rocket throws up his palms in a peaceful gesture.

"We cool, Butch. We cool. What's going on with you?" Rocket says as he stands at a respectful distance but Butch doesn't respond. "Look, I know you're upset about your friend. I'm not like his celly. You don't have to ever worry about me. I'm straight. Ain't shit another man can do for me but die in my place. You're a good kid. I know you're hurt and confused. Look, I didn't even try to get you to sleep on the bottom bunk. I don't want anything from you but to be able to sleep peacefully around you. Right now, I am not sure if either of us can sleep in here now. We have to work this out. I'm not like that," Rocket says.

Butch sighs, "We cool. I'm just tripping off of all of this. Man, he a good dude...Man, I have sent eight letters out and nobody wrote me back yet. I'm pissed. How they going to just say fuck me? I did what I could for everybody. When I shot that cop, I was on my way to drop off twenty five hundred to my Auntie so she could get the bathroom re-done in her house. Now she saying fuck me too! She been there all my life. She the one who raised me after moms died. I know she struggling but a stamp? She can't buy a damn stamp? She the reason I started hustling... Her ass went out on disability because she fell at the job and messed her back up. Who was there for her? Me! That's who. Her little checks from social security and whatever welfare gave her couldn't pay her mortgage on that damn house. I stepped up! I was the man of the house so it was my responsibility. I'm telling you, Rocket. I got on that block and stayed there until I was making six thousand a month. She didn't want for shit. Now she can't even write me? Shit. Her and all those damn friends that supposed to care about me don't give a fuck about me! Where they at now when I need them? Why the fuck everybody keeps leaving me! First my pops left.

Then my moms died. Now, my Auntie, my girl, or none of my damn friends write to me or come and see me! I set over that jail for years and got three visits! I live like twenty minutes away, Rocket! Where are those people who supposed to love me? And now I'm sitting in prison because I shot a dirty cop that made his overtime by robbing the dudes on the block! Ain't no justice! Where is my justice, Rocket? I feel like nobody loves me. I ain't even get a letter from my damn Auntie. Rocket, and the last letter I sent her, I included a stamped envelope! I still ain't got no response." he whimpers.

Rocket sighs. "I know it's hard, Butch. Prison lets you in on the truth about everything. You learn that you wasted your life to buy love and material things that don't last or love you back. Don't allow this to make you bitter. You can't win being angry in here. Anger will convince you that it will go away if you can just find somebody to take it out on. You're stronger than that. You have to be, Butch. The one suggestion that I will make is that you take this time to figure out what you're going to do with the rest of your life. You don't have long before you're free and living it. You're a young man. You can get out of here and really live like you have never done. All you have to do is walk away from all of that bullshit you were doing on the street. That shit led you here. You got another shot to do good with yourself. Don't let not getting any mail break you. I look for mail everyday and it's been over two decades. I just be hoping for somebody to think enough of me to send me something. I don't care if it's an empty envelope. I would appreciate the fact that they thought of me. But I'll never let that break me. Damn, Butch, now I'm feeling bad for you and my damn self. Together, we'll work this out," Rocket says, laughing.

"How you figure that?" Butch inquires.

"Shit. I'll write you and you write me back," Rocket replies. They start laughing, but sadness remains in both of their eyes.

Chapter 28

Rakeys is lying on the top bunk reading a law book. Sherman is seated indian style on his bunk reading a newspaper. The door way goes dark as Susan steps in front of it. She counts them as they look toward her. She retrieves three pieces of mail with Sherman's name on it off the top of her stack of mail. Then she taps the bars with the mail.

"Mr. Ford, you have mail," she says with a hint of disappointment in her voice. He walks over to the bars. She stares angrily at the two cards and the regular envelope after seeing they were from Ella. She glares at him. "This has to stop," she says as she hands them to him.

He looks at Ella's name, "Stop?" he says.

"I'm serious, Mr. Ford, this will be considered contraband from now on if I am delivering it. I'ma return it to sender," she says seriously.

He sighs. "Don't do that," he says before looking over his shoulder at Rakeys. Rakeys is staring at them. "That's my man from The Hill."

"I don't remember him," she says.

"I was in the hole for eight years," Rakeys says.

"I hope you learned your lesson?" she shouted back, dismissively.

"What in the fuck does that suppose to mean?" he says with some irritation in his voice as he drops his book and scoots forward.

She whispers to Sherman, "Are you going to allow him to talk to me like that?"

"She alright, Ra'," Sherman says.

Rakeys sighs and lies back on his pillow. He mumbles, "Cracker".

Susan smiles and whispers, "You do care."

Sherman shakes his head. Then she hands him a thick envelope and taps it with the tips of her fingers. He looks in it and sees a hunting knife. He smiles, "You do care" he whispers. They both grin.

"Excuse me." Rakeys shouts.

"Yes, Sir," she replies.

"Why are we on lockdown," Rakeys asks.

"Someone hung himself in the shower," she says emotionless. He shakes his head and starts reading his book.

"You all will be on lock down until tomorrow. I'm working over here tonight. I'll stop by later and you're welcome," she says before walking halfway away from the cell. She stops and catches Sherman before he could walk back to his bunk. "Mr. Ford," she says.

"Yea," he says.

She points at the mail. "Remember from now on that is contraband. Have I made myself clear?" she says seriously. He smirks and walks away. She walks off of the tier.

"Wussup with her?" Rakeys questions.

"She's a cool chic. She's just looking for love in all the wrong places. I can't give her what she really wants. Right now she's just a means to an end," Sherman replies as he walks toward his bunk.

"What kind of ends?" Rakeys says with a smile that says sex.

"That too, but more importantly, this," Sherman says as he opens the envelope for Rakeys to see the knife.

"Damnnnnn. I need me one of those. Get her to get another one," Rakeys says as he lies back down.

"Naw. She'll feel like a flunky then...If I make parole, see if you can pull her," Sherman replies.

"When you make parole! You have to speak it into existence. But, back to me. Do I have to pay to get some play from her?" Rakeys inquires.

"Naw. She operates off love. It's strange tho, she looking for love in prison," Sherman says with a puzzled look.

"Sheed," say Rakeys, "You have women who only date dudes locked up. I guess they think if they can prove to the dude that they'll be with him during his worst of times, that the dude will become devoted. My problem with the shit is, I can't find me one of those broads. I'm looking for love. I write poetry and all of that soft shit. Sheed. I'll even do some off key singing for her ass. But, it's dudes like you with girlfriends and wives that find these damn women. A motherfucker like me that is looking and willing to pay for some attention, can't get shit. So, I'm left with porn magazines. Now the administration wants to take those because sometimes I kiss and occasionally lick the chics on the pages. They petty asses don't want me to have no damn pleasure unless it's with a damn man. I don't get down like that. They can keep that AIDs shit. They can take my books, but as long as they don't take my Baby Oil and imagination, I'ma beat it until the skin comes off. And when it grows back, I'ma beat it again. Anyway, how do I get this white girl?" Rakeys questions.

"I think if you wait, she'll come to you. She wants me to be her man but that won't happen. When I leave here, I'm leaving all of this shit behind. I'ma keep in contact with you and a few other dudes but that's it. I hate that I'ma hurt her feelings but I'm not leaving my woman. So, she'll probably come to you complaining about how wrong and dirty I am. You just listen. Sooner or later, she'll offer you something," Sherman says as he sits down on his bunk.

"All I want is to see that white cherry blossom so I can pluck it," Rakeys says as they both laugh.

"I'ma get into this mail. Hopefully, they clean up the showers and let us out. I need to take one," Sherman says before he opens one of his letters.

"Hold on, Sherman, I have to get some shit off my chest. I just realized what these motherfuckers are doing to me," Rakeys says as he pops back up in bed. "Damn. Do motherfuckers ever just take a damn shower back there?! I been in here 24 hours now and two motherfuckers are dead in the showers! Whatever happened to just washing your ass in there? Why the shower has to be the last place a motherfucker wants to be caught at? I know one of these trifling motherfuckers started this bullshit. Ain't no asses getting clean in here," he shouts as he jumps off of the bunk and walks over to the bars and screams on the tier, "I'ma wash my ass even if I have to kill a motherfucker to do it," Rakeys barks before turning to Sherman shaking his head in disappointment.

"I hope that wasn't the little dude Blue Eyes," Sherman says with a hint of sadness.

Chapter 29

BH Bandit has one side of his head against the cell bars as he concentrates on listening to Rakeys rambling. He starts giggling.

Yesterday is seated at the top end of his bed. He's staring at the side of BH Bandit's head with a look of irritation. "Get the fuck a-w-a-y from the cell door," he snaps.

"What? Who the fuck you think you talking to, Youngsta?" BH Bandit snaps as he turns to face Yesterday. Yesterday leaps off of the bunk with his fist clenched.

"You, Bitch! You heard what the fuck I said. Say something! Say anything and I'ma beat yo ass up in here," Yesterday fumes. BH Bandit throws his palms in the air in surrender.

"Youngsta, you got it. I don't want no static," BH Bandit pleads.

"What did I tell you my mothafuckun name is?" Yesterday says through clenched teeth.

"Yesterday. You're name is Yesterday. I just say youngsta because you're younger than I am. I don't mean no harm. From now on, I'ma call you by your name," BH Bandit continues to plead.

Yesterday starts jabbing his finger in front of the man's face. "You ain't going to call me shit. Don't ever say my name. I want your faggot ass out of my cell as soon as the doors pop," Yesterday says.

"Man, I ain't no mother-," Yesterday interrupts his speech with a smack across the man's face. BH Bandit motions to ball up his fist but reconsiders and cowards into a stooping position. "Man, I'm fifty three years old. I don't want no violence."

Chapter 30

Around 1:00am Blue Eye's eases off the bottom end of his bunk. Big Bob's eyes pop open. He pretends to be asleep but he's peeking at Blue Eyes. Blue Eyes eases his sheet off of the bed. He whimpers lightly as he steps on top of the toilet and ties one end of the sheet around his neck. He eases the tip of one corner of the sheet through a slit in the solid vent above the toilet and pulls it through another slit until most of the tip is through. He takes the longer end and wraps it around one of the bed posts until it's tight. He ties that end into a knot. He double checks the end that is tied around his neck to make sure it is tight before stepping up and planting his feet on the sink. He closes his eyes in prayer. Tears start pouring down his face. Big Bob leaps up and slams his fist into Blue Eye's belly and swiftly punches him across his chin with his other hand. Blue Eyes crashes into the mirror above the sink. Then Big Bob starts punching him furiously across his whole upper body causing him to slip. The sheet begins strangling him. Big Bob lifts him up and tosses him on top of the sink. He holds him by his neck with one hand to prevent further strangulation as he continues to beat him with his free hand. Blue Eyes swings his fist wildly but with no real energy because the sheet and the man's fist are close to strangling him. Big Bob pins the man by his neck to the wall mirror and uses his freehand to scoot the end of the sheet that is tied to the bed post off of the post. Then he grips the middle of the sheet around his fist and punches Blue Eyes in his stomach before tossing him onto the floor in between the bed and the toilet. He starts pounding him with both of his fist as Blue Eyes desperately tries to shield himself from the blows. Then Big Bob grabs him by the back of his neck and pins him down flat on his stomach across the floor. He pulls on the sheet to tighten it further around Blue Eyes' throat to prevent him from screaming. He rips Blue Eyes' pants down and rapes him.

Chapter 31

5:00am morning, the cells doors begin to screech partially open and slamming closed. Then after the sixth time the doors remain open.

"Chow time, Gentlemen," Susan screams from the guards area. Rakeys and Sherman get up. Rakeys retrieves his knife from under his mattress and climbs down off of the bunk. The two start getting dressed. A few minutes later John and Big Moe come and block the cell door. Rakeys snatches his knife free. Big Moe smiles.

"Those are my folks," Sherman says to Rakeys as he blocks him with his arm.

"My apologies, men," Rakeys says as he puts his knife back into his waist.

"No problem. It's good to see you're on point," John replies. "I'm John and this is Big Moe".

"Rakeys is the name, " Rakeys replies. "Sherman, are you going to breakfast"?

"Ya walking down?" Sherman asks Big Moe and John.

"You know I wanna eat," Big Moe says with a huge smile as he rubs his belly.

"We wanna holla at you though," John says.

Rakeys knows that means that he isn't welcome to walk with them. "Sherman, I'll see you there," Rakeys said before stepping out of the cell.

Big Moe, John, and Sherman trail Rakeys down the tier. Sherman glares at Susan before her smile freezes in shock.

The four men walk onto the crowded compound. Psycho walks past them back into the cell block. Other men are walking toward the kitchen or lingering on the walkway. They barely notice Skip and seven other Aryan Brothers standing on the walkway. Black Smoke and Dre are facing Marc. Marc is faking as if he is holding a conversation

with them but he's really watching the
Aryan Brothers.

"You know those white boys are getting
all of the money on the compound. They
controlling these niggas like slaves.
They smiling in their faces like they love
them, knowing these crackers will cut
their throats and spit on their corpses.
Sherman, we can get this money. It ain't
like on The Hill. These dudes have
bigger demons, they need dope to keep
them spaced out. So, man, I need you
to reach out to your connect so we can
get it jumping out here," John says. "We
moving on up to heroin, Champ".

"John, I have to think about that, "
Sherman says.

"You have to think about it?" John says
with a hint of hostility in his voice.

"Yea," Sherman says firmly.

"What's there to think about? Either you
in or you're not. We can make some
serious money in this spot," John says
casually.

"I"m getting ready to go up for the board again," Sherman says.

"The board? Fuck the parole board," John says bitterly.

Sherman stops. John stops and smiles. Big Moe stops ahead of them.

"I didn't mean it like that, Sherm. I'm just saying that they ain't going to know about this. Shit, me and Big Moe can keep the shit so you'll be safe," John says smiling.

"Let me think about it," Sherman says before walking passed them. John frowns at Big Moe. Big Moe hunches his shoulders and they join him up the walkway.

Chapter 32

"Excuse me, Officer," Psycho respectfully says as he enters the building. He stands near the gate to the tier and the larger gate that separates the guards from the prisoners. Susan is on the other side of the room looking through the gate onto the Lower B-tier.

"Doors closing in two minutes! Chow time, Gentlemen," she says before looking over to Psycho. She then motions him to hold up. Psycho tenses and positions his back to the guard's gate as Larry and four other men walk past him to the exit. Larry glances at him but non-threateningly. A few other men walk past Psycho as Susan screams down to the Lower A tier. She then walks over to him. She seems a little irritated.

"No, you can't come on this block if you don't live here. Other than that, how can I help you?" she says.

He smiles, "I do live on A-Upper. I'm sorry. Good morning, sister. I see you're a little irritated so I will be brief," he says as she sighs. "One of our brothers needs to be moved to a cell that is more...comfortable for his well-being," he says before pausing to study her facial expressions.

"One of OUR brothers?" she replies quizzically.

"White brothers. He's in a cell...if I can be blunt...with a despicable nigger and everyday that he remains in that environment threatens his health, safety and ability to comfortably do his time. This place is stressful enough, and I would be eternally grateful if you would grant OUR brother a cell change," Psycho says as he continues to study her facial expressions.

"I have no brothers in here," she says before walking over to her desk and rambling through a few folders before pulling a sheet of paper from one. She walks back over to him and holds up the front of the paper for him to see. "This is a cell change request form. Have your Brother fill this out, return it back to me and I will make sure it gets to the Captain for review.

Thirty seconds of silence passes as they stare into each others eyes. He fights his irritation as he continues to try to study her. She looks with annoyance.

"Are you a sympathizer?" Psycho asks.

"Sympathizer?" she questions.

"I know we haven't had an opportunity to become acquainted. But I only want to keep our Caucasian brothers safe, unified, and men. Sister, I am sure you can see with your very own eyes the danger that exist in this environment for Caucasian men. We're outnumbered 100 to 1. We're hated by every non-white person in here because we tried to humanize and provide these savages an opportunity to become humane, dignified, and God fearing. We both know the senseless crimes and all the problems of the world exist because these THINGS are incapable of anything but acts of cruelty and destruction. As a white man, it is my responsibility to protect our brothers in here because we are always at war. As a Caucasian woman, it is my responsibility to protect you as well in this environment where they all fantasize of being me. So they seek to conquer you by any means. Sister, I need you. The white race needs you. I call upon you to do everything in your power to remove our brother from out of that cell with this animal before we have to slay the beast. We will not allow him to defile our brother," Psycho genuinely pleads.

She shows him the paper again. "This is the process to have your brother moved to another cell. Since you believe he will be defiled, I can have him moved to protective custody. What's his name?" she replies.

Psycho sighs. "No thank you, my White Princess. I see you don't understand the depths of the situation. I pray to our Lord that this isn't because you are a nigger lover," he sincerely says.

"What did you call me?" she snaps.

"Princess, I didn't call you anything. I merely said, 'I hope you are not a nigger

lover'. Good day," he turns and walks
out of the door.

Chapter 33

Blue Eyes is leaning with his back against the far wall from his cell door. He is fully dressed and he has his shoes tied tight. His head is tilted back with his eyes closed. There is a cold determination in his stance. His head slowly begins bouncing as he balls his fist and begins to sway from the rhythm in his head.

"And if I die, I'ma die on my motherfucking feet. Neva make a bitch of me. I was built on the streets, I was raised on the streets, and I'ma kill any motherfucker that eva comes against me. Cause if i die, I'ma die on my motherfucking feet. Neva make a bitch of me," he raps calmly but with intensity to himself.

Suga comes and stands in the cell doorway. "Excuse me, Blue?" he says softly.

Blue Eyes' eyes slowly open as he stares sinisterly at him, "What?"

Suga steps further into the cell. Blue Eyes stands in defense with his fist at his side.

"I come in peace. If you want this madness to end, you have to slaughter him. It's the only way that the rapes will stop and the rest of the compound will respect you. You can't let it go any further. I'm not trying to tell you what to do but I know this isn't who you are. You're a man. A real man. So, it's time to prove it to yourself and the rest of these motherfuckers who doubt how gangsta you are," Suga says firmly.

Big Bob walks into the cell and rubs Suga across his ear with his free hand. He has a sandwich wrapped in a paper towel in the other hand. "Glad to see ya ladies conversing," he says as he steps in between them. He winks at Blue Eyes before turning his smile on Suga. "Can you please show her how to wear that eyeliner? I love that."

Suga smiles. Then Big Bob puts the sandwich on Blue Eyes' bed and gets naked in front of them. He grabs his towel and wraps it around his waist.

He smiles at Suga, "I am a faithful man. Sorry. My Suga is right there. Right, baby?" he says before blowing Blue Eyes a kiss and walking to the showers.

Suga shakes his head in regret, "Here." He pulls a small and narrow shank from his waist and holds it out toward him. The shank is small enough to be concealed in the palm of his hand. " I know it's small but it'll do what you need done. Go for his heart, temple, juggler or cut his nuts from underneath of him," Suga says as he points to each location. "The best way for you to do this is for you to go in as if you want to be intimate. So, I advise that you keep the knife hidden in your palm. The handle in the center of your palm and the blade along the back of your wrist. If you go at him that way, he'll let you get close. Then stab him where you want. Where ever you stab him, keep sticking until he stops moving. If you hit him in the temple, press down hard and slice hard. Don't let him survive or he'll come for you. He is a brutal bastard".

As Blue Eyes grabs the shank, Yesterday steps into the cell. "What the fuck you doing in here with my mothafuckun main man?" Yesterday snaps as he reaches for his shank. Suga spins around, throws his palms in the air to block any shank slashes and steps backwards.

"Yesterday, he's cool," Blue Eyes says. Yesterday looks at Blue Eyes then to Suga. Then he looks back to Blue Eyes. He steps out of the path of Suga. Suga briskly exits the cell. "You ok?" Yesterday says with genuine concern as he extends his hand. Blue Eyes grips his hands and they hug like buddies. "Fuck these prison rules. I fuck with you, Shawty. I'ma see if I can get you in my cell today or I'ma slaughter this bitch nigga for you. We ain't having this shit no longer. Fuck all these bitch ass dudes. You hear me? Fuck dat, I'ma just smash him. Where the fuck he at?"

Blue Eyes starts giggles. "Let me handle this, Cuzzo."

"You sure? Cause you haven't been handling it to my satisfaction so far," Yesterday says.

"I got it," Blue Eyes says with conviction.

"Today," Yesterday demands.

Blue Eyes nods in agreement. "Today," he confidently says.

Then Yesterday shakes his hand and hugs him again. "Bet. I'm getting ready to let my cell buddy know he's moving out today so you can move in with me. I'll be back in a few minutes," Yesterday confides. Then he exists the cell.

Blue Eyes takes all of his clothes off except his boxers. He put his boots back on and ties them tight. He grabs his shower gear and shank and goes to the shower.

Big Bob is rotating his back underneath the shower water. He smiles when he sees Blue Eyes enter, "Welcome, baby. I love taking showers with my boo. Come here. Come here. I want a hug," he says. Blue Eyes smiles. Big Bob opens his arms for a hug. Blue Eyes walks into his arms. He tried to hug him around his neck but Big Bob hugged him around his neck instead. He kisses him on the top of his head. Then he holds him by his cheeks and stares in his eyes, " I'm going to take care of you. No more rough stuff. From now on, I'mma make lov--," he said before catching a glimpse of the shank in Blue Eyes' hand. He immediately turns his upper body to the side as Blue Eyes swings the blade for his temple, but stabs him in the side of his head. He stretches his upper body back as he tries to hold him at bay. Blue Eyes continues to swing, cut and slice whatever he can reach. He's rapidly stabbing Big Bob's arms. Big Bob eases his hands around Blue Eyes' neck and begins choking him. Blue Eye's continues to swing until his body is drained of its energy. His arms drop to his side but he continues to hold the shank in his hand.

"Go to sleep, Baby. That's right, Baby," Big Bob whispers cooingly to him. He leans in as Blue Eyes' eyes flutter. Blue Eyes slams his forehead into the man's nose. Big Bob shoves him backwards as he grabs his own bleeding and broken nose. Blue Eyes springs back onto him and begins to stab him rapidly in his arms, upper body and face.

Big Bob starts running from him. Blue Eyes stays on his trail stabbing him in his back and shoulder until the injured man starts slowing down. Big Bob stumbles and grabs hold of the bars of the first cell as he enters the tier. Butch, Rakeys, Sherman and a group of other men pause as they watch Blue Eyes start stabbing him in his side and head as Big Bob swings behind him, desperately trying to fight him off of him. He drops to one knee and starts swinging more wildly.

Yesterday appears behind Blue Eyes as Big Bob's body crashes to the floor. Blue Eyes stabs him wildly in the back of the head before leaping up and starts stomping him with his feet. He goes back to stabbing.

"Lock down! Lock Down!" Susan screams from behind the guard's gate.

"This is Yesterday! This is Yesterday! Come on, Blue! Come on, Blue! We have to go," Yesterday grabs him by his waist and pulls him off of the man as he calmly talks to him. "It's Yesterday".

"Lock down! Lock down!" Susan continues to scream from her safe place.

"I have to make sure he's dead," Blue Eyes shouts.

"He's dead. He's dead," Yesterday calmly says as he pulls him into the showers. He points to the shower that Big Bob was using. "Rinse off. Hurry up. Give me the knife," he says.

As Blue Eyes follows his instructions, Blue Eyes begins to recite, "And if I die, I'ma die on my motherfucking feet. Neva make a bitch of me. I was built on the streets, I was raised on the streets, and I'ma kill any motherfucker that eva comes against me."

"What?" Yesterday looks into Blue Eyes' strange but focused eyes. Blue Eyes' voice is calm as if he doesn't have a care in the world. Blue Eyes continues to recite the rap. "You did good, youngsta. You did good. Stay right there," Yesterday goes and peeps on the tier. He sees there are only prisoners on the tier. Most of them are moving as quickly as they can to their cells. He turns back to Blue Eyes. "Come on! Hurry up. Grab your clothes!" He ushers Blue Eyes onto the tier. "Get in your cell, dry off, put your clothes on and get in bed and pretend to be asleep, " he says.

"Lock down! Lock down! Now! Now!" she continues to scream. The majority of the men are off the tier but in their doorways. Sherman looks at her. Then he looks and sees Big Bob moving. He looks back at her. Sherman runs down the tier screaming.

"He needs help! Get this man some help!" he screams as he slides on his knees. His body stops in front of Big Bob's head, blocking Susan's view of the body. He wraps one of his arms around Big Bob's neck and holds his other hand over Big Bob's mouth and nose. He begins to use all of his strength to twist his head as hard as he could until his neck snaps. He continues

to hold his hand over Big Bob's mouth
and nose as he looks over his shoulder
at Susan and screams, "He needs help!
He's dying! He's dying!"

*Susan buzzes twenty officers
onto the tier.*

Chapter 34

Butch starts laughing in Rocket's frustrated face after Butch slams an ace of spade down on Rocket's queen of spade causing Rocket to lose the game. Rocket slings the cards onto the floor. "Shit. Gotdamnit! How in the hell you keep that?" Rocket angrily says as he pops up and walks to the cell door. "Shit!" he shouts onto the tier.

"Stop all that screaming on my tier, Jail Birds!" Sergeant Jackson screams as he steps onto the tier.

Voices from cells all over the cell block shout, "Fuck you!"

"No fuck ya! I'll send all this damn mail back! Say fuck me one more time. I dare you," Sergeant Jackson shouts. Silence all over the tier.

"Sergeant Jackson, come on man, I'm waiting for mail from my mommy," Psycho screams.

"Well, ya betta learn to stay in ya place! Respect your superior and I thought you killed your mother, Jail Bird," Sergeant Jackson says jokingly.

"Heyyyyyyy, watch your mouth! That's my mommy," Psycho says seriously.

"Ok, Jail Birds, mail call and count time! I have a lot of mail here for the ones that are still loved. The rest of you abandoned assholes, I'm just counting you," Sergeant Jackson shouts.

He steps in front of Rakeys' cell. Rakeys is taking a shit on the toilet, "You better not be beating your dick, Motherfucker. I don't play homosexual games, faggot," Sergeant Jackson says jokingly to him.

"Sarge, I don't play like that. You joke with these other dudes but respect me like I respect you," Rakeys says seriously.

"Man, fuck youuuuuuuuuu. Your cell buddy is still in the hole for murder, I see. That's what happens when idiots start thinking for themselves. I guess he'll be in the hole for ten years. I thought the fool was going home soon. I guess he didn't want to go home," Sergeant Jackson says as he shakes his head and walking off. He passes other cells until he stops in front of Butch's cell. Rocket is still standing in front of it. "Get your big ass out of my way. I need to see your cell buddy".

"Did I get any mail?" Rocket says with pleading eyes as he steps against the wall so Sergeant Jackson can count Butch.

"No. You know don't nobody love you," Sergeant Jackson says as he continues to joke with the prisoners.

"Fuck you! How would you like it if I rip your motherfucking head off your fucking shoulders, bitch ass motherfucker?" Rocket screams in rage.

Sergeant Jackson smirks as he continues his journey down the hall. Very few men in the entire block received any mail. Some yell out in frustration.

"You ok?" Butch says as he stands.

"Yea. Yea. I mean, no. I'm tired of this fucking shit! How can my people just say fuck me?" Rocket says as he grips and pulls on the bars in frustration.

"I know your pain. I didn't get shit either," Butch says reassuringly.

Rocket looks over his shoulder at him. "You don't understand, Butch. I told you I haven't received any kind of mail from my people for over two fucking decades. That shit rips me apart every fucking time they pass out mail so that's five days a week for over two decades. You can't possibly understand my pain. Plus, you're getting ready to go home so you'll be back with your people soon. I'm dying right here. Every fucking day I lose more hope because these fuckers don't even send me a fucking birthday card. What the fuck am I living for? I have life in here. I don't get visits. I don't get my phone calls accepted. Fuck, all the numbers are changed and I don't get a fucking letter from nobody in my family. I have two brothers and two sisters who are still alive. They haven't even sent me a picture of their kids when they were babies. What the fuck am I living for? I'm just waiting to die. I suffer everyday, youngsta. You have been the most joy I have had since being in this damn place and you getting ready to go home. Why in the fuck do they put you short timers in here with us lifers? They shouldn't do that but I guess that's what they want, to fucking tease us," he says sadly. Then he faces the cell and screams out onto the tier, "Well, ya have fucking accomplished it! Ya satisfied?!"

"Shut that damn screaming up on my tier," Sergeant Jackson says from the second floor.

"Fuck you," Rocket screams.

"You know I'll write you when I go home," Butch says.

Rocket turns to him. "You'll write me for the first month. Then you'll go on with your life just like everyone else," Rocket says before sighing.

Chapter 35

It's 1:00am. Rakeys appears in his doorway seconds after the cell doors start opening. He looks over to Sergeant Jackson who is standing with his fingers on the switches to open the gates and cells. He is staring at Blue Eyes and Sherman as they wait for him to hit the switch to unlock the gate that leads to the tier.

"Mr. Ford, I see you got away with another one," Sergeant Jackson says sarcastically.

"I didn't get away with shit," Sherman replies.

Sergeant Jackson hits the switch and Blue Eyes pushes the gate open and they walk to the tier.

"Heyyyyyyyyyyyy! Blue Eyes!!! Wussup, young gangsta," Rakeys says as he steps on the tier to shake Blue Eyes' hand. Blue Eyes smiles proudly.

Men around the tier begin to shout his name like he is the new superhero. He smiles.

"Shut that damn noise up or ya will not come off lockdown today! Rakeys get your ass back in that cell! You two killers get ya asses off of my tier...now!" Sergeant Jackson barks.

Sherman shakes Rakeys hand before they step into their cell. Blue Eyes starts walking to his cell.

"Blue," Butch shouts from his cell.

Blue Eyes runs down to Butch's cell. Rocket is standing in the background. Butch extends his hand through the bars.

"Wussup, Cuzzo," Blue Eyes says.

"Glad you're back, Blue. These bamas on the whole compound been hollering about how gangsta you are. You handled your business. It's a new day,"

Butch says proudly to him. Rocket is trying to reassure him as he nods confirmation in the background.

"From now on, it's on. I don't give a fuck who it is, they can get it, Cuzzo!" Blue Eyes says with a frightening determination.

"Get yo ass off my damn tier or I'll ship your ass back to the hole," Sergeant Jackson screams.

"Let me get in this cell, Cuzzo" Blue Eyes says as he shakes his friend's hand before running down to his cell.

Chapter 36

It's 5:00am.

"Jail birds, I am getting ready to open the doors for chow! Doors will stay open for five minutes! Be ready. You are now off of lockdown! Unfortunately for you, I am doing overtime! Make me mad and your asses will be back on lockdown! Enjoy your breakfast," Sergeant Jackson screams as he flicks the switches to start opening the cell doors.

The prisoners cautiously look onto the tier before walking onto it. Suga and Nancy are the first men to appear from the upper level onto the bottom tier. Suga leads the way as they stop in front of Blue Eyes' cell. Blue Eyes spins toward them with a look of rage in his eyes before calming down.

"What?" he says impatiently.

"First, I wanted to congratulate you. You handled your business. The second thing I wanted to do is offer you our services," Suga says in a playful tone.

"What the fuck ya want?" Yesterday fumes as he walks up behind them.

Nancy and Suga are so consumed with fear that they don't even look behind them at Yesterday.

"Speak before I put these knives in ya confused mothafuckas," Yesterday barks as he slips two shanks from his waist.

"I-I-I-I. We we we we we. Oh God," Suga stutters.

"Hold on, Cuzzo. Let me hear what they have to say," Blue Eyes says to Yesterday. He can't see Yesterday because of Suga's huge frame.

"Fuck dat. Ain't shit they got to say beneficial to you. They think you're they girlfriend or some shit. I'm killing every mothafucka that is disrespectful to you," Yesterday fumes.

Suga finally turns toward Yesterday as Yesterday takes a step toward Nancy. Nancy is trembling. "Hold on, Mr. Yesterday. We just wanted to tell Blue Eyes that we will supply him with as many shanks as he can use. Nancy here makes them," Suga blurts.

Yesterday pauses. "What?" Yesterday says in complete shock.

Nancy faces him and smiles but it quickly vanishes. Then he lowers his eyes. "Yes. I make most of the shanks on the compound," Nancy says.

"She even made the knife Blue Eyes used to kill his celly," Suga adds.

Yesterday grips his knife as his eyes go more sinister, "What in the fuck you just say?"

"I mean. I mean. I meant, the the the. I-I-I gave Blue Eyes a shank. No I-I-I didn't. I-I didn't give him anything," Suga stutters, "Look we we we don't want any problems. We just want to give you knives."

"I don't want your mothafuckun knives. Get the fuck away from us... NOW!" Yesterday orders.

The two homosexuals briskly walk off of the tier. Blue Eyes shakes his head and smiles at Yesterday. "You have some serious issues, Cuzzo" he says.

"Fuck that. Blue, you know what happened to you. You can't have them hanging around you after you got these MEN respecting you now. The further you keep them hoes away from you, the better," Yesterday warns.

"We can use the knife connect, Cuzzo" Blue Eyes says.

"Oh, we goin to get the knives but we aint those motherfuckers friends. I still don't trust them. They get a lot of shit started in prison. Plus, they killers. They ain't in here for bad decorations. I heard Nancy is more vicious than most of the straight men on the compound. I was told he was doing hits on the street and in Occoquan. Plus I heard the dude Suga snapped some dudes neck over a drug deal and then shot him twenty one times before cutting off his dick. Yea, he's a real dick eater. So don't let that fake

scared shit fool you. Keep them out of
your face. Let me deal with them,"
Yesterday warns.

Chapter 37

Two months later, Susan is driving down a narrow and dimly lit street. She parks in front of a small brick house. The street is lined with identical looking houses on both sides of the street. She gets out and goes and knocks on the house with the uncovered glowing porch light. She knocks. A few minutes later the peep hole gets dark before the door's top and bottom locks are heard unlocking. Ella opens the door in her robe. She smiles a nervous smile.

"Hey, Girl," Susan says, "I'm sorry for coming by so late. Can I come in?"

Ella's face shows fear. "Is everything alright? My letters have been returning and every time I call the prison they won't tell me anything. It's been so hard for me to get up there. I used all of my leave. Susan, please tell me he is ok," she asked with concern.

Susan smiles again. "He is fine. He's been going through a lot, but he's healthy and not in the hole," Susan says reassuringly.

Ella sighs in relief. Then she steps aside. "Well, come on in," Ella says.

Susan walks into the house. In her pajamas, Loretta comes half asleep down the staircase and stops in front of the last step.

"Hey sleepy girl," Susan coos.

Loretta comes alive and rushes over to hug her. "Hiiiiiiii, Aunt Susan," the child gushes.

Susan squeezes her tight and rocks her before kissing her on her cheek.

Ella looks at Loretta. "What are you doing down here? I put you to bed an hour ago. You should be asleep," Ella says with very little emotion.

"I heard the door, Mommy," Loretta responded.

"Well, it's been answered. Now go to bed and I don't want to hear, Mommmmy, I'm tired when I get you up for school. Night, Loretta," Ella says.

Susan's bottom lip drops and she looks disappointedly at Loretta. "I'll come by and see you soon. Ok?" she says.

Loretta smiles and hugs her again. "Ok...Bye, Mommy," Loretta says.

"Goodnight," Ella says as the two women watch Loretta disappear up the stairs. Then Ella looks at Susan, "Kids. They'll find any reason to stay up. Would you like something to drink?"

"I'm fine. I just came to talk to you. This should have been done a long time ago," Susan says.

Ella leads her to the small dining room table. Susan takes a seat while Ella goes and grabs two bottles of water. She hands Susan a bottle before sitting. "What's this about? You ok?" she says with concern.

Susan stares at her briefly before looking down at her fumbling hands. Ella reaches out and tries to comfort her by rubbing the top of her knuckles. "You can talk to me. What you say will not leave this room. Are you ok, Susan?" Ella asks.

Susan sighs. Then she looks into Ella's eyes before dropping her hands into her lap. She sighs. "Sherman isn't in love with you any more, that's why he has been sending your letters back. He says he is tired of leading you on. He says he cares about you but he never loved you. He does love his daughter that's why he has tolerated you but now he can't keep pretending," Susan says before pausing to watch Ella fall apart.

"Whhhhy? I don't understand," Ella says with tears pouring down her face, "This can't be true. I know he loves me. Why would you come and say these things to me? Whhhhhy?" Ella pleads.

"Because it's true. I respect you and don't want to see you putting your life on hold any longer for a man that doesn't want you. Let him go. Just let him go.

He said that he won't accept anymore of your letters. He'll refuse your visits and he's not going to call you. Ella, just move on. I know there is some guy out here who you are interested in. Give yourself a chance. Give him a chance. You deserve to be happy," Susan says.

"Some guy? What? I am faithful to my man. Why would you say this to me? You should know me good enough to know I would never do that. What's really going on, Susan," Ella says.

Susan sighs. She coughs into her hand. " I hate to be the bearer of this kind of news but it's the truth," Susan says. "I have to get home. It's getting late. I just didn't want you to keep worrying. Ella, you are a beautiful, intelligent and caring woman. You'll find the man for you in no time. Don't even sweat it, girl," Susan says as she gets up and walks towards the door.

Ella wipes her tears from her eyes, but they continue to fall as she walks with Susan to the door.

Susan hugs her and wipes tears from the woman's eyes. "You'll be just fine. Watch. Just know you are a good woman. Don't allow Loretta to see you in so much pain. Be strong for the both of you. You're such an amazing mother. You'll find your Prince. Just let Sherman go. It's what he wants and what you need. Ok?" she says before kissing her on the cheek and begins walking down the steps.

"Is he your man now, Susan?" Ella says. Susan pauses. Then she starts walking around to the driver's side of her car. "Susan!" Ella shouts.

Susan gets in the car and drives off.

Chapter 38

*Blue Eyes and Yesterday follow
the crowd out of the unit onto the
compound. They are headed up the
walkway toward the kitchen. The
compound is crawling with prisoners
and a few guards sprinkled around the
perimeter.*

"So your Mom's a cracker. I mean. I'm
sorry, Blue. Force of habit. So your
Mom's white?" Yesterday says sincerely.

Blue Eyes adjust his hidden
shank in his pants that is slipping. "Yea.
So, I got my eyes from my Moms. Every
since I can remember dudes have been
testing me either because my Moms
white or I got blue eyes and the chicks
digging me. So, I've been fighting all my
life to prove I'm not no soft ass pretty
boy," Blue Eyes says before quickly
shaking a man's hand that is walking
past.

"You are a pretty boy. Those eyes make
you exotic to black women. All the black
chicks want their babies to have pretty

hair or colorful eyes. Even though I think you're a ugly mothafucka, the chicks dig you. They probably been trying to fuck you since you could walk. The sad part is you ain't got to be worth shit. You got those eyes or that hair, it's like you ain't all nigga. This shit crazy. Because I'm one of the smoothest mothafuckus on the planet and I get money, but a bitch will choose you over me," Yesterday yelps.

"That's what the fuck I'm talking about, Cuzzo. That's why I been fighting all my damn life because of that shit you just said. Dudes mad at me because I was born with these eyes, Cuzzo," Blue Eyes says with excitement because of the confirmation.

"Shit. That shit gives unfair field advantage," Yesterday says jokingly.

Blue Eyes sees Skip with tattoos all over his face. He's standing on the side of the walkway with Psycho and three other Aryans. "All these damn eyes do is see, Cuzzo," Blue Eyes says pointing to his eyes. "I'm still a nigga in everybody's eyes. The white boys don't treat me no better and I am half white, Cuzzo," he says, laughing.

"Well, you don't have to prove yourself on this compound. You done proved yourself," Yesterday says reassuringly.

"That's how that bullshit with Big Bob happened because of these eyes," Blue Eyes says seriously as they walk into the kitchen.

"That shit ain't neva happened. You push that shit out of your head," Yesterday says as they step into the back of the short line. There are three men ahead of them getting food put on their plates. After Blue Eyes and Yesterday grab their food, they go and sit down on opposite sides of each other. There is space for two men on one side of Blue Eyes.

"So, Rakeys is going to help you give some time back," Blue Eyes asks.

"Yea. I'm hoping I can get a new trial. Fuck giving some time back. I want to give it all back. I'm like that nigga on Amistad. "Set me free," They both laugh.

"The dude is good tho. The only thing I can't understand with jail house lawyers is that they can help everybody else go home or give some time back but themselves. That shit is crazy," Yesterday says shaking his head.

Mitch comes and sits straddled across the bench facing Blue Eyes. He smiles as he rubs his own groin and licks his lips. Both Blue Eyes and Yesterday pause and stare at the man.

"Hey, Blue Eyes. How you doing?" Mitch says in a cooing voice.

"Uh? Blue Eyes says.

Mitch licks his lips and leans within inches from Blue Eyes' cheek. "I was wondering if...If you...um. Damn. You smell good," he says as his lust filled eyes stare into Blue Eyes' eyes. "Your scent and the fact that I am sitting so close to you is...uh...uh. Making my body respond. Look, I want you to move in my cell. I know you're tired of all the drama you getting caught up in out here. I'll protect you, Bab-"

Blue Eyes jams his shank into Mitch's heart before he could finish his sentence. Yesterday immediately leans over the table and stabs the man in his neck. They briskly walk out of the building with the rest of the prisoners. Mitch is crouched over dead at the table.

Chapter 39

Two days later Sherman's cell door slides open and Blue Eyes, Rakeys and Yesterday come walking on the tier at 6:00am. Sherman steps in the doorway fully dressed.

"Weeeeeeeeeeeee're backkkk," Yesterday shouts jokingly before shaking Sherman's hand and hugging him. "Wuuuuussuuuup, Partna, another one down. We beating beefs like we're farmers," he says as he giggles.

Rakeys pats him on the shoulder as he slides passed him into the cell. Blue Eyes shakes Sherman's hand after Yesterday steps away from him.

"Hold up. Hold up. All three of ya, let me holla at ya for a minute," Sherman says seriously. They follow him into the cell. Yesterday leans over with his elbow on the sink and his backside on the wall. Blue Eyes stands with his back against the open cell door. Rakeys jumps up on his bunk. He takes his shoes off as he looks at Sherman.

"Men, ya have to chill out. Ya involved in too much shit. Ya been in the hole four times in two months over some petty shit like this last dude stepping on your shoes, Yesterday? Come on, that middle school shit. That shit could have gotten ya put on permanent lockdown. Ya can't keep stabbing and killing dudes and don't expect any repercussions either from these dudes or the administration," Sherman warns.

"Man, the dudes can come at me any time they want. Sherm, you talking like we just starting shit. Situations coming to us. And as far as the dude stepping on my shoes, that shit hurt my feet. Man, I have tender toes. Plus, he drew his weapon. Now as for the administration, fuck the police. I'm already locked down. The hole ain't nothing but another mothafucking cell. I'm home wherever they send me, Sherm, I don't have no parole or release date. Plus, I ain't letting these dudes violate. I'ma keep on digging that knife in them, Sherm. You know I ain't on no gangster shit. I'm all about peace, my brother," Yesterday says smiling.

Sherman just shakes his head. Then he stares at Blue Eyes. Blue Eyes looks toward the door then back at Sherman. Then he lowers his eyes. "Blue, come on, Shawty. You done stabbed eleven motherfuckers and four of them died. Everybody know you a man. You got their respect. You don't have to prove nothing now. Look, I know you had to smash the first dude," Sherman says before Blue Eyes interrupts him.

"What about the dude that asked me for some ass in the kitchen, Cuzzo?" Blue Eyes says staring blankly into Sherman's eyes.

'Ok. I can understand you having to [7]put some work in on that one, but everything else could have been avoided. Blue, when you roll on someone you have these two crazy

_____

[7]

Note: "Put some work in" and "Roll on someone" means to stab or attack someone.

motherfuckers following right behind you."

"Yesss siiirrrr," Yesterday jokingly says.

"Fo'real, Yesterday," Sherman says looking him seriously in his eyes. Yesterday's smile vanishes and he nods his head. "All I am saying is that everybody on the compound know ya killers so they're going to stay out of your way. Ya can stop this wild shit. And you," he says pointing up at Rakeys, "You suppose to be the jail house lawyer helping yourself and them give all this damn time back. How you going to be working on cases from the hole?" Sherman says.

"I hear what you're saying, Sherm, but you also know we new over here and these dudes need to know we aint having it. Statements need to be made," Rakeys says.

Sherman shakes his head in disappointment. "Well, ok, all of the statements needed to be made have been made, right?" he says as he looks at each of them.

"Naw," Rakeys responds.

"Who else is left? Who are you beefing with now?" Sherman asks.

"What about them bitch ass niggas John and Big Moe? I told you that I be hearing little shit. The nigga whispering that he put that knife in you, but he's acting like he fucks with you in your face. So how are you going to handle that?" Rakeys questions.

"What? Cuzzo, I know you focused on going home. I'll handle both of them for you, Cuzzo" Blue Eyes says calmly.

"No. Don't go at them. Look, I'm not worried about John. I got that under control," Sherman says.

"Sherm, you can't sleep on them dudes. Them dudes are putting the press on most of the dudes on the compound. Motherfuckers are terrified of them. Sherm, I just don't want them [8]rocking

---

[8] Note: "Rocking you to sleep" means to act as if there is no problem but secretly trying to harm the unsuspecting person.

you to sleep. Lets get them before they get you. I'm telling you they are just smiling in your face," Rakeys warns.

"I got them," Sherman says sharply.

Rakeys nods his head as he smirks.

"All you have to do is give the word and we'll handle it, Cuzzo" Blue Eyes says.

Sherman's cell door starts opening and closing.

"All you jail birds that don't live in that cell, get the fuck out...now," Sergeant Jackson shouts from behind the guard's gate.

Chapter 40

Two days later the cells open for lunch. Men start exiting their cells and the tier. Rakeys waits for Yesterday to exit his and Blue Eyes' cell. They leave the tier.

Butch jumps off his bunk and puts on his shoes. Rocket is still lying on the bed on his back. His hands are behind his head and his eyes are wide open. Butch taps him on his elbow.

"You going to get something to eat?" Butch asks with a hint of concern.

"No," Rocket mumbles.

"You alright?" Butch inquires.

Rocket sighs. "I'm just feeling a little down."

"Wussup? Spit it out," Butch jokingly says.

"You're a good dude. You're the best pain in the ass celly I have ever had.

You've really grown on me. I'ma miss you when you're gone. I really am. So, that's what got me down. I just realized that my old ass is still going to die here." Rocket responded.

"You know Rakeys is a beast at helping dudes give some of their time back if not all of it. You should let him look over your case. You want me to holler at him for you," Butch says with excitement.

Rocket sits up. "My case is so old. Only person probably still alive is me. The judge and the rest of them probably died years ago."

"Shit. That should make it easier for you to get out. I say shoot your shot, if it doesn't work, I'll fly a helicopter over this damn place and pull you up," Butch says as they both laugh.

Rocket stands and shakes his head. "Just remember, Butch, that you can still do a lot of good with your life. You have a good heart. We all made some mistakes but you can start fresh. Just know this old man learned a lot from you and appreciates your wise counsel. To be honest, I don't want to see you go because that'll mean I'm still here. Then they will probably find the biggest asshole that they can to put in here with me. I'm tired of fighting. I'm tired of fighting black men, white men, Latinos, the courts, the guards and everybody else who wants to fight. So, do you really think Rakeys will help out an old man?" Rocket says smiling.

"You're not old. You're healthier and can probably out pace everybody in this place, but yea, I think he'll help. I know he will. I'll even pay him," Butch says.

"Naw. You don't have to do that. I have a few of those pennies saved that they pay us every month. Talk to him for me," Rocket says with excitement. "I'm following you home if I don't beat you there!"

They both laugh. Then the cell doors begin to shake.

"Go ahead. I'ma eat me some Ramen Noodles tonight, but first I'ma wash these sheets in the sink. So, don't think the sheet is up because I am taking a dump. They'll be drying" Rocket says smiling.

Butch exits the cell and walks down to Blue Eyes' cell. A few seconds later Blue Eyes exit the cell and the two men walk toward the exit of the tier.

As Butch and Blue Eyes exit the tier, heading to the kitchen, Black Smoke, Dre and Marc come walking from the shower area. Black Smoke signals them to wait for him by the showers. He then walks down to Skip's cell. Skip and Razor are fully dressed and appear to be getting ready to leave the cell. Black Smoke knocks on the frame of the cell. Both Aryan Brothers look at him in the doorway. Razor frowns before pretending to wipe his mouth but he's actually spitting a razor blade into his hand that was hidden on the left side of his mouth. Razor takes an aggressive step toward Black Smoke. Skip is close behind them.

Skip's face is now tatted with eleven Aryan tattoos. One of the tattoos is a tear drop dangling from the corner of his left eye. His eyebrows have been

shaved and he has the words "White" on
one brow and "Power" on the other
brow.

"Yesssssssss," Razor says sarcastically as he stands in attack mode.

Black Smoke smiles, "I just want to do some business. You know what I'm saying?"

"Business?" Razor says with a look of confusion as he scans the man.

Psycho walks casually past Dre' and Marc. Bear is close behind him. He stares both of the black men in their eyes with a daring look as he passes them.The two Aryans stop behind Black Smoke at a respectful distance, "How can I help you, Brothaaaa," Psycho says with his hands on his waist.

Black Smoke looks over his
shoulder and frowns at Psycho but he
quickly relaxes and moves from in
between the four men. Dre and Marc
have moved closer but at a respectable
distance. Both men visibly have their

hands near their knives hidden in the
waist of their pants.

"Psycho, "I'm trying to buy some work.
You know what I'm saying," Black
Smoke says.

"How much," Psycho replies.

"Seven grams of heroin. You know what
I'm saying," Black Smoke says
confidently.

"You know that's going to cost you three
grand," Psycho says.

"I can handle that. You know what I'm
saying," Black Smoke says smiling.

"No. I don't. But we're out at the
moment, we'll be back in business next
week. I'll let you know when we have it,"
Psycho says with a look that reads, get
lost.

Black Smoke smiles, nods his
head and walks passed the cells toward
the front of the tier with his crew close
behind him. They don't even notice
Rocket's huge frame standing on top of

the sink near the doorway. He has one end of the wet sheet rigged on the vent with the other end tied tightly around the bedpost. He checks the end tied around his neck to make sure it's tight. One end of a thick strip from a pillowcase is tied around his wrist. The other end is fastened into a loop big enough for a smaller hand to fit in. The loop dangles. Once he is satisfied with the tightness of the sheet around his neck, he places his hands behind his back and forces his big hand into the loop. He tugs to test its durability before stepping off of the sink. The sheet tugs and begins to strangle him. He tosses and turns but can't break free of the strip that has his hands tied. His feet kick wildly toward the toilet seat. He has changed his mind but death didn't listen. His body begins to convulse as he pisses on his self and blood starts trickling down his nose and mouth. His eyes open into a death stare of regret as urine drips from the bottom of his pants.

Chapter 41

Four days later, Blue Eyes and Butch are walking up the compound toward the recreation yard. Blue Eyes' confidence increases and his stride, as countless men acknowledge him. He nods his head in their direction but keeps his attention on Butch.

"Damn. So your celly hung himself in the cell? How in the hell did he tie his hands behind his back and hang himself?" Blue Eyes asks.

"I guess he tied the sheet around his neck first after he hooked it to the wall. Then I'm assuming he tied his hands with scraps of sheet after he stood up on the sink and jumped," Butch says.

Blue Eyes shakes his head and smiles. "You're very descriptive not to have been there, Cuzzo".

"You sound like the Administration. That's why they put me in the hole! Now the parole board will probably deny me parole," Butch says sadly.

"Naw. They figured out the dude hung himself, that's why your ass is walking the compound. You good. Your crying ass will make parole, Cuzzo." Blue Eyes says reassuringly.

Butch smiles but it quickly vanishes. "I hope so. Man, Rocket was a good dude. He smiled a lot but the dude was really depressed and I think me getting ready to go home took him over the edge. He was just tired of being alone. His family cut him off over two decades ago. He didn't get no mail. He couldn't call anybody because they changed their numbers after his Mom's died over fifteen years ago. I didn't know he was going to go out like that because I would have talked him out of it. The man taught me a lot about this place, but I can imagine how he must of felt. Imagine being locked up over two decades and nobody from the outside world reaches out to you" Butch says in remorse.

"I don't have to imagine that, Cuzzo. I'ma live that," Blue Eyes says in almost a whisper.

"I promise you, when I get on my feet, I will help you get a lawyer," Butch says.

"Anyway, I'm mentally preparing myself for whatever happens. But damn. Yea. He was cool. I remember when I was going through that shit, he would drop me off some food from the kitchen. He didn't say shit but, 'I'ma leave you this on the sink. Be strong, young brotha'. I never had a chance to thank him, you know? I remember one of those times I was in the hole, two dudes hung themselves and they left notes talking about they were tired. They couldn't do any more time," Blue Eyes says.

Butch shakes his head, "Man, this place ain't no joke. It's a damn shame that people you thought loved you on the outside will kick you to the curb. Shit. People stopped writing and coming to see me over the jail right after I got my time. They said fuck me. The only person who I could call was my Auntie and now I can't even call her. Damn phone is disconnected...Blue, you have to cut this bullshit out and try to give this time back."

"I am. Rakeys is nice with them appeals. He helped two dudes on The Hill give life sentences back and that's not counting all the dudes he helped give shorter time back or have a reduction in their sentences. He looked over my shit and said that I have a few good issues that he can work with. And check this out, he was just scanning when he told me that! So you know when he really looks into it, I'ma be good. I'ma get out of here in probably 2 or 3 years, Cuzzo," Blue Eyes says confidently.

"Cool. All I'm saying is that you have to chill out with all of this beefing and stabbing dudes and shit before you catch another case. If you catch a body and get life, then those issues he's finding won't be worth shit. You can give your time back but you'll have another life sentence to deal with. Just chill out, Blue. Don't lose sight of the streets. I know you frustrated and angry but don't give up on freedom," Butch said.

"I won't. Trust me, I won't, Cuzzo" Blue Eyes says.

Chapter 42

Rakeys and Yesterday are seated across from each other in the dining room. There are over two hundred and fifty men either eating, getting their food, exiting, or entering the kitchen. Big Moe and John have just finished getting their food trays. John spots Rakeys and nods his head toward him. Big Moe follows him over to Rakeys.

"Slim, can I get your seat?" John says to the man seated next to Rakeys. The man's frown vanishes as soon as he looks behind him and sees that it's John and Big Moe. He nods his head in agreement, as he and the guy next to him go find another seat. John looks at Rakeys who is still eating and not paying him any attention. "Can I sit here?" John asks Rakeys as Big Moe sits down.

"Sure," Rakeys says without looking at him. Yesterday is staring at John as he puts food in his mouth but doesn't chew. As John takes his seat, Big Moe starts eating and scanning the kitchen. He sees BH Bandit and Albert sitting with Nancy and Suga.

"How you feeling, Rakeys?" John asks with sincerity.

"I'm good," Rakeys says dryly.

"Wussup, young gangsta! Man, I am hearing all of the work ya are putting in," John says to Yesterday with excitement.

"I ain't no gangsta. I'ma praying man. All I want is peace and harmony, Brotha," Yesterday says with a straight face.

John smiles and shakes his head. Then he focuses on Rakeys, "Where's Sherman?"

Rakeys looks John in the eyes, "I don't know where he's at," he says before continuing the last bit of food on his plate.

"Do we have a problem," John says in an almost threatening tone.

Rakeys looks him in his eyes, "I'm good. You have a problem with me?"

John smirks. "Naw. All I got is love for you but you seem a little irritated by my presence."

"Hmm. I'm just not in a talkative mood," Rakeys says.

"I can respect that," John says.

Then Rakeys and Yesterday get up and walk their trays over to the tray rack.

"Do you want to smash both of them right now? Fuck them. We can slice their mothafuckun throats right here," Yesterday says with excited and determined eyes.

"Naw." Sherman said, "Don't touch them."

Yesterday smirks as they both exit the kitchen.

"Hey Bandit and Albert, come here," John says as the two men along with Nancy and Suga were leaving the tray rack. Albert and BH Bandit walk over to John. Suga and Nancy stand back in the distance but within eavesdropping range.

"Wussup, John," BH Bandit says as the two men shake John and Big Moe's hand.

"I need a favor," John says.

"Anything. What's up?" Albert says.

"I want ya to get rid of Sherman's little crew. Then I want both of ya to fuck Sherman real good for me. I'm trying to put the press on him but it's hard to get in ya block. Can ya help me out?" John says.

"Yes. I want to do something big with Yesterday anyway. I was only holding off because I knew you had a relationship with them. Consider that handled," BH Bandit says.

John shakes their hands before the men walk out of the kitchen.

"John, why would you do that to Sherman?" Big Moe asks with disappointment.

"That man basically said fuck us. You see he didn't get that shit in here yet. We been waiting for two months. I let that sucka live on this compound long enough. You know I haven't forgiven him for killing my brotha anyway. Fuck that nigga, Moe. Who you with?" John asks seriously.

"The man is getting ready to go home. I can understand and respect he doesn't want to take any chances," Big Moe replies.

"Fuck him going home. We ain't going no fucking where. Why should I have sympathy for him!? Fuck that sucka. He should of died when I tried to kill his bitch ass before. So don't come at me with that feeling sorry for that hoe. And after they fuck him, I know he's going to kill those fucking faggots then guess what? He in here with us for life. I bet he'll get them drugs on the compound for us then. You and that feeling sorry for him shit," John says fuming.

Chapter 43

Yesterday and Butch are standing in front of Butch's cell talking. Inmates are coming back from the kitchen walking to their cells or hanging out on the tier. BH Bandit is trailing behind Albert, Suga, and Nancy as they passes Butch and Yesterday. Then BH Bandit walks past and bumps into Yesterday. He doesn't apologize. He just keeps walking.

"Your sucka ass didn't see me standing here," Yesterday shouts at him. BH Bandit walks up and punches Yesterday in the face. Yesterday falls into the wall. Bandit follows up with a slew of punches.

"Don't nobody jump in this," Yesterday shouts as he tries to block some of the blows. He is hitting Yesterday with some powerful shots that are hurting him. Yesterday swings back. The men on the tier eagerly watch. Butch watches with his fist clenched.

"Back up, bitch, back up to the showers!" Yesterday shouts to BH Bandit before launching a punch that doesn't land. BH Bandit follows up with a body shot and a punch to his head. Yesterday stumbles to the wall.

"Lock down! Lock down," Susan screams from behind the guards' gate. She can't see who's fighting because the prisoners are intentionally blocking her view.

Rakeys and Sherman run onto the tier.

"Don't nobody jump in! This is mine," Yesterday continues to shout. "Back up to the showers, mothafucka."

Yesterday swings and misses again. BH Bandit rams his shoulder into Yesterday's body and slams his back into the wall. Yesterday groans but he immediately starts punching the man in his body and head. BH Bandit drops to one knee. Yesterday follows with punches to the side of his ear and face. BH Bandit wraps his arms tightly around Yesterday's ankles and uses all of his

*strength to lift him off of his feet.
Yesterday stops swinging and starts
trying to hold his balance and pull at one
of the man's ears. When Blue Eyes
steps out of the cell, he instantly
snatches his shank from his waist and
stabs BH Bandit three times in his side.
BH Bandit releases Yesterday.
Yesterday quickly snatches Blue Eyes
away from him as he was moving swiftly
to kill him.*

"Lock down! Lock down now! The ERT
is on its way," Susan screams as the cell
doors shake

"This is my fight, dammit," Yesterday
shouts.

Blue Eyes stares him in his eyes.
"Fuck that! If I can't kill him, you can't
fight him either, Cuzzo!" Blue Eyes
shouts in a rage.

The cell doors shake again. "Lock
down! Lock down! The fight is on lower
A. I'll buzz ya in now," Susan shouts to
the emergency response team as they
enter the building.

Butch steps up to them. "Get him later. ERT is in the building," he says as he pushes them toward their cell. They lock in.

After the guards have the tier locked down, they make each man remove his shirt and searches them for fresh bruises. They handcuff Yesterday and take a badly bleeding BH Bandit to the hospital. Susan tells ERT that she thinks Rakeys was involved. Even though he disputes it, they lock him up too.

Chapter 44

It's 11:00pm. All of the prisoners are locked in their cells. Susan checks the switches to the cells and doors to make sure all of the cells are closed and the entrance doors are locked. She removes her keys from her belt and opens Sherman's cell before she unlocks the gate that leads to A-Lower tier. Sherman steps into the cell door. She holds her finger over her lips to shush him and waves him back in the cell. She walks on to the tier. She knows there are prisoners up against their cell doors but they are further down the tier where they can't see her.

She walks into the cell. "Plant your back against the wall. This is a shake down," she says loud enough for those that can hear her. He does as he is told. She immediately begins to kiss him. He kisses her back as she pulls down his pants. He spins her around and plants the front of her body to the wall as he pulls down her already unbuttoned pants. He slips his erection inside of her from the back. She moans.

She begins to bounce against him. He leans in and kisses the back of her neck and her ear as he grinds inside of her.

"You know Rakeys didn't have anything to do with that fight," he whispers in her ear.

"How else was I going to get in here tonight? I'll let the Captain know I made a mistake tomorrow. They'll let him out. Now shut up," she says as she pulls him out of her and turns to him. She kneels and begins to give him the best head he has ever had.

He stumbles backwards and ends up awkwardly seated on the edge of his bed. She pushes him in to a lying position. She continues to give him head as she removes her pants and straddles him.

Chapter 45

Sergeant Jackson hits the switch that unlocks the exit door. Yesterday enters the building. He stops and pushes at the locked gate that leads to the tier. He looks over to Sergeant Jackson who is staring at him.

"Sergeant, are you going to let me in or what?" Yesterday says with no aggression.

The Sergeant walks casually over to him. "Are you tired yet?" Sergeant Jackson asks.

"Yea. I'm trying to get in this cell and get some sleep," Yesterday says jokingly.

Sergeant Jackson holds on to the gate. "I've seen a lot of tough guys die back here. Shit, I've seen a lot of men who don't want any trouble die back here. Sooner or later you're going to get tired of the violence or either you're going to get too old for this nonsense. You don't want to create too many enemies because you'll never be able to quit. I've seen it. You can't win every time. Everybody's luck runs out and we all die. I just want you to think about it," Sergeant Jackson says before hitting the switch to unlock the door.

Yesterday walks on to the tier, "I'm backkkkkkkkkkkkkkk," he shouts on the tier before stopping at Sherman's cell. Sherman is brushing his teeth. Rakeys is lying on his bunk and reading a law book. "Wussup, men?" Yesterday says.

Sherman spits the toothpaste out of his mouth while Rakeys sits up. "Wussup? I see you beat another case. You back for good?" Sherman says smiling.

"Depends on these chumps. That faggot ass Captain held me in the hole for two weeks even though that faggot bandit told him it wasn't me...Anyway, you went up for parole yet?" Yesterday asks.

"I go up tomorrow," Sherman replies.

"I know you're tired, but walk with us to chow. I found some technicalities in your case that I think can get you a new trial?" Rakeys says with excitement.

"For real? What! Yea. I'm walking wit'cha," Yesterday says with excitement.

"Get the hell off of my tier, Jail Bird!" Sergeant Jackson shouts. Then he flickers the switches and the cell doors open and close, "Chow time! Chow time! Doors will close in five minutes."

"Let me wash my face and I'll be back down," Yesterday says.

"We'll wait for you," Rakeys responds.

"Naw. I'll catch ya in the kitchen," Yesterday says before walking down to the open cell that he shares with Blue Eyes. He steps into the cell and stares at his sleeping cellmate.

"Blue! Wussup? I'm back!" Yesterday shouts excitedly.

Blue Eyes looks over at him with one eye. "Good for you. I'll holler at you when I get up, Cuzzo" he says before going back to sleep.

"Man, you know you suppose to be up when these doors open! You slipping, Blue," Yesterday says seriously.

"Yesterday," Black Smoke says from the cell door licking his lips and rubbing his hands. When Yesterday looks at him, he nods his head toward the back of the tier. Yesterday follows him through the crowd of men exiting the back of the tier. He follows him to the showers area where Marc and Dre' are leaning against the wall.

"Wussup?" Yesterday asks with curiosity.

"Man, those crackers got an ounce of heroin yesterday. You know what I'm saying? They suppose to cut it up today. You know what I'm saying? Look, it's in there with Skip. Razor and the rest of them already left for breakfast. You know what I'm saying? If we're going to get that we have to go now. You know what I'm saying? I'm serious. You in?"

Black Smoke says with urgency as he licks his lips and rubs his hands.

"I'm in. Let me go and get strapped," Yesterday replies.

Black Smoke pulls out an icepick and hands it to him.

"Lets go," Yesterday says as he spins around and briskly walks toward Skip's cell. Black Smoke signals Marc and Dre' not to move. They don't move. Black Smoke smiles with a look of satisfaction as he licks his lips and rubs his hands.

Yesterday runs into the cell. Razor is seated on the bottom bunk tying his shoes. Skip is finishing up taking a piss. Yesterday doesn't see him and runs passed him toward Razor but Skip blindsides him with a punch to the face as Yesterday raises his icepick to stab Razor. Yesterday tumbles to the wall. Razor grabs Yesterday's hand that holds the icepick and slams it against the rail. The icepick drops and Skip snatches it. Yesterday immediately starts punching Razor. Razor blocks his face with one hand and spits a razor out of his mouth into his other hand. Skip stabs Yesterday in the side before Razor slices him across his face with the razor. A deep cut spreads open below his left eye and across his nose to the beginning of his right cheek. He kicks Razor backwards and shoves Skip away from him. He turns and runs out of the cell. Running at full speed through the crowd of men, he desperately tries to make his way to the front of the tier. Skip is on his heels and repeatedly jamming the icepick into Yesterday's upper back. Yesterday collapses in front of Sherman's and Rakeys cell as Sergeant Jackson immediately starts closing the cells before anyone else could get out. The men on the tier start squeezing into anybody's closing cell door, leaving Skip and Yesterday on the tier. Skip continues stabbing him as his body starts to convulse before lying lifeless.

Rakeys stabs Skip in the shoulder from inside his cell."Get the fuck off of him," Rakeys shouts frantically.

Skip moves out of Rakeys' reach and continues to stab Yesterday. He then plunges the icepick into Yesterday's side and neck. Blood squirts into his face and chest. He blinks repeatedly trying to get the blood out of his eye before raising the icepick above his head.

"Get off of him, Donavon!" Sergeant Jackson screams.

Skip jams the icepick down into Yesterday's face and leaving it sticking out of his cheek as blood squirts into the air and onto his body. Then he grabs the dead man by his feet and starts dragging him up and down the tier screaming, "White Power" with his fist pumping in the air. A trail of blood is smeared across the floor. Blue Eyes, Butch, Sherman and Rakeys are desperately trying to rip their cell doors open.

The other Aryan Brothers shout along with Skip, "White Power" on to the tier. The ERT runs onto the tier. Skip releases the body, gets down on his knees and clamps his hands behind his head before the guards get to him. He has an insane look in his eyes with Yesterday's blood drying and running down the front of his body.

Chapter 46

Sherman places his hands on his knees under the table to try to keep them from shaking. He immediately starts tapping his feet uncontrollably as he stares at the collar bone of the Caucasian man seated across from him in his freshly cleaned three piece suit. Mr. Clark is the man's name. He is seated directly across the table from Sherman. Mr. Clark is reading from a folder with a stack of papers inside. Two women in business attire are seated on opposite sides of Mr. Clark. Mrs. Kingston, a Caucasian woman, is staring at Sherman's trembling shoulders. Mrs. Washington, an African American woman is watching his forehead because she can't fully see his eyes. Mr. Patterson, a Caucasian man, with a button down shirt and old slacks is pacing behind his co-workers and staring at Sherman. Standing behind Sherman but on opposite sides of him near the door are two Corporals. Their eyes are focused on him.

"Most recently you spent one year in solitary confinement after a stabbing that pierced your heart-" Mr. Clark says before being interrupted.

"Put your hands on the table, Mr. Ford," Mr. Patterson orders.

Sherman's knees immediately begin to shake as he puts his trembling hands on the table. He presses his knees together to stop them from moving. He starts toying with his ears with his fingers to prevent everyone from seeing his hands shake.

"Put your hands on the table, Mr. Ford," Mr. Patterson says again.

Sherman does as he is told. He sighs. He starts rubbing his hands and randomly scratching his arm.

"Can you stop all of that moving. You're making me nervous," Mr. Patterson says.

Sherman clinches his fingers together in front of him.

"Mr. Ford, for a man with such a short prison sentence compared to all the others, you have been in some major incidents. What did you do to get stabbed," Mr. Clark questions.

"I didn't do anything. I peeked onto the tier and saw all of the rioting. I tried to make it to the guard's booth so I wouldn't be accused of being involved in the riot. Somebody stabbed me before I could get there. There wasn't any altercation or anything," Sherman replied.

"I see when you first arrived at Occoquan your shoes were taken from you. Tell me about that?" Mr. Clark questions as Mr. Patterson goes and stands behind Sherman.

"My shoes weren't taken. The shoes were old and stinky. I left them in the holding cell at the jail. The guards just didn't notice that I didn't have any on until I got to Occoquan." Sherman replies.

" Are your parents alive?" Mrs. Washington asks.

"My father isn't. My mother just moved into a senior's medical facility," Sherman says as he fumbles with his fingers.

"Is she ok?" Mrs. Washington asks.

"She has heart problems and she's a diabetic," Sherman replies.

"Well, Mr. Ford, I am not sure if I can honestly say you are ready to be released," Mr. Clark says as Sherman's heart starts pounding. "However, we have to decide this as a team. Can you please step out of the room? We'll call you back in when we have made a decision. It should take us a few minutes," Mr. Clark says as he signals Sherman to stand.

Sherman staggers a bit as he stands. He sighs. "I just want ya to know that I really don't belong here. I made a few mistakes in my past, but I've learned from those mistakes. I just want to go home and be a productive member of my community and be a father and husband to my soon to be wife. I know ya are aware of how angry a lot of these guys are. Sometimes violence erupts for no apparent reason. I'm not one of those angry guys. You're right, compared to most of the men here, I don't have a lot of time. I have everything to lose and nothing to gain by getting in trouble. I'm not a troublemaker and I am not the same guy I was when I got arrested. I hope ya will take into account that I haven't had one incident since being here. I even tried to save a man's life," Sherman says remorsefully.

"Thank you, Mr. Ford. We'll call you back in when we're ready," Mr. Clark says.

Butch is seated amongst four other prisoners scheduled for their hearing today. There are two rows of chairs where the men are scattered around. Butch is seated in the middle of the first row. He is a complete nervous wreck. He watches his patting foot and mumbles to himself what he plans to say to the hearing officer. A guard is filling out paperwork off to one side of the room.

Sherman exiting the room breaks up the silence. All of the prisoners look at him and the two guards trailing behind him. One of the guards taps him on his shoulder and points to where Butch and the others are seated. Sherman nods his head to Butch. Butch stares quizzically at Sherman as he goes and sits behind him.

"They denied you?" Butch says with a look of fear.

"Not yet. They told me to step out the room. It doesn't look good tho," Sherman says in a drained voice. His feet are still tapping.

"I hope they give it to you. Did they seem upset?" Butch quizzes.

"They really didn't show any emotions," Sherman replies.

"Were you scared," Butch questions with his own fear very visible.

"Naw," Sherman says before clenching his mouth after his teeth chatter. His foot starts tapping faster. He looks down at them. Then he crosses his leg and sits back.

"We'll, I'm scared as shit. I know they'll probably deny me. Shit I shot a cop," Butch confides.

The door to the parole hearing opens and Mrs. Kingston appears. She scans the men. Then she spots Sherman. "Mr. Ford, we're ready for you now."

Sherman was about to speak but his teeth chattered so he decided to keep his mouth closed. His legs are wobbly as he stands. He sighs as Butch looks over at him.

"Good luck," Butch says.

Sherman smirks before walking into the room behind her. The two guards follow him back into the room. Sherman walks toward his chair as the last guard closes the door. Mr. Patterson motions Sherman to stop. Mr. Patterson is standing behind his co-workers. Mrs. Kingston retakes her seat. Then she looks into Sherman's eyes. He lowers his head.

"Look at me, Mr. Ford," Mrs. Kingston says. He does. "This was a very hard decision for us to come to."

Sherman's heart is pounding. He grips the back of the chair for balance but looks as if he isn't worried.

"Trouble seems to find you, Mr. Ford. Incident after incident," She says.

"But I never was-" he said before she interrupted him by holding up her palm.

"We have to worry about the safety of the community. It is our responsibility to make sure you are no longer a threat to society. Clearly you had a very difficult upbringing. It's also apparent that trouble finds you or you follow it. We haven't been able to figure that out because the majority of your incident reports were caused by someone else..." she says.

Sherman feels his fear turning into anger. He grips the back of his chair harder.

"Because of the majority of the incidents being no fault of your own and because we are aware of the level of violence that takes place here, we see that you have been able to stay out of trouble the best you could. So, Mr. Ford, we have decided to grant you immediate parole. It may take a couple of days for your paperwork to be processed but you will be a free man in days," she says without a smile. None of her co-workers smiled.

Sherman's face turned into a huge smile! He reached over the table and shook all of their hands.

"Don't make a fool out of us, Mr. Ford," Mr. Patterson says.

"I won't," Sherman replies as the guard taps him on the shoulder and escorts him out of the room.

He looks at the anticipation in the faces of the prisoners waiting to see the parole board. Butch's eyes are full of fear. Sherman smiles at him. A huge smile surfaces across Butch's face as if he just made parole.

The guard at the desk speaks into the receiver of the phone on top of the desk as Sherman walks over to Butch.

"Man, so they're in a good mood? Huh?" Butch says with excitement.

"I guess so," Sherman replies.

"They have to be because you was messing up before you got over here, right? And they still gave you parole," Butch says.

"I guess," Sherman replies.

Captain Dewitt walks into the room with three other officers following behind him. Captain Dewitt is an overweight Caucasian man with blonde and graying hair. The officers follow him over to the desk where another officer is doing the paperwork. The prisoners watch them closely. The officer pointed to Sherman.

Sherman and Butch tense up as the Captain approaches. "Mr. Ford, I need to have a word with you".

"What's this about?" Sherman says while watching the other officers with suspicion as they stand behind him.

"I assure you that everything is alright. I just want to have a word with you," Captain Dewitt responds. Then he turns and starts walking in the direction he came.

Butch looks at Sherman with hesitation.

"You'll be fine. I'll see you back on the block," Sherman tells Butch before following the Captain. The other officers follow close behind Sherman.

Chapter 47

A long conference table divides four lower-ranking officers from John, Big Moe, Psycho and Slaughter House. The officers are standing against the wall near the door. There is one empty chair with a file in front of it on the table. Big Moe and John are seated next to each other with their chairs turned to a slant, facing the Aryans. The two Aryan Brothers are standing near the other end of the table conversing.

They all look to the door as Sherman steps into the room with Captain Dewitt and the other officers. All of the prisoners look at him with suspicion.

"Wussup, Sherman," Johns says in a tone that indicates skepticism.

Sherman hunches his shoulders. Big Moe stands and shakes and hugs Sherman.

"What's this about?" Sherman says to Big Moe.

The Captain takes a seat opposite them. "Gentlemen, I brought you all here because I need your help. I'm trying to prevent a race riot and since you are all [9]shot callers, you are my go to guys," Captain Dewitt says.

"You have the wrong dude. Can I go back to my block?" John says as he motions to stand.

The Captain signals him to stop. "Please, we're not going to go down this road. I'm not in the mood. So, let me make my proposition. Then you can go back to your cell. Deal?" Captain Dewitt continues. "Now, there was a killing in 2 block on A lower between an Aryan and a Black man. Both men are affiliated with you guys. I want the violence to end there. This is what I am offering each of you for your assistance. One, you will receive four extra visits for the next four months. Two, you will be allowed to make six phone calls a month for the next six months on a secure line in the

---

[9] "Shot Callers" are men in prison who have influence over other prisoners and are classified by the administration as leaders of gangs.

Chaplain's office. Your phone calls can last for one hour. And three, you can be assigned to any work detail of your choice except for outside details for trustees. My portion of the deal will take effect today...I'm going to keep the prison on lockdown for two more days so whatever you tell your guys will sink in. Now if you refuse or are unable to stop any racial violence or tension, I will find a dark damp corner in the hole and place each of you in separate corners for the next ten years. You will not have any human contact outside of my officers. There will be no one hour recreation, no phone calls, no visits, and no mail. Plus I ax any frivolous medical requests. You will have to be near death to be seen by a physician and that will take place in your cell. In addition to all of this, you will receive a disciplinary hearing by me for every incident that takes place and I will find you guilty. You will be sentenced to additional time in the hole. All of this will be overseen in-house. There will be no outside criminal charges filed. Gentlemen, you will rot away in the hole. Those of you who know me know I am a man of my word. Now, these officers are here to take you to every block on this compound so you can talk to everyone you need to talk to so you can end the retaliations. Good day, Gentlemen.

Captain Dewitt immediately exists the room.

Chapter 48

Sherman is seated on the edge of his bed, writing a letter to Ella. Rakeys is lying on his bed with his head propped up on his pillow. He's reading a law book and there are four other open law books along him. John steps up to the closed cell door.

"Sherm," John says.

Both men in the cell look at him.

"Let me holla at you. Rakeys, wussup, Champ," John says as the cell door opens. Rakeys nods his head toward him but goes back to reading.

Sherman exits the cell. John leans on the wall opposite the cell doors but not directly in front of the cell. Sherman spots Big Moe talking to Blue Eyes through the closed cell door and Slaughter House talking to Razor through Razor's closed cell door. Sherman leans on the wall opposite John.

"How is everybody?" John says.

"They understand," Sherman replies.

"I heard you didn't take a detail," John says with a cunning look.

" I don't need one," Sherman replies.

"Sherman, I thought we put that shit behind us. Man, I know you made parole two days ago. You know there aren't any secrets in this spot, but you try to keep them from your friends. How do I suppose to take that?" John says.

"I don't know how you supposed to take it. However, I wasn't hiding it," Sherman says staring directly in his eyes.

John smiles. "It's cool. So when do you get released?"

"I'm waiting for the paperwork to come back," Sherman replies.

"That takes like a week. I'm actually happy for you. Sherm, you were never made for this place. You need to be out there with your family."

"What in the fuck does that mean, John?" Sherman says with irritation.

John starts laughing. "I didn't mean it like that. I meant, you a good dude. This place should never be your home. Me, it's a different story. Anyway, I'm happy for you. Can I ask you something?" John says watching Sherman's eyes.

"Wussup?" Sherman replies.

"What's your plan?" John asks seriously.

"Getting home to my family," Sherman sincerely replies.

" I mean, are you going to become a square or you getting back into the streets," John says.

"I'm becoming a square," Sherman says smiling.

"I feel you. Look, I can use your connect. I'm sure they won't mess with me because they don't know me so can you connect us? Let them know I am a cool dude. I can get the drugs in. Shit. I am cleaning the compound now. Give me a few days and I'll have a tie into one of the trustees that works on the other side of the wall. Once I get one of them under my wing, they'll bring the drugs straight to me. No risk for you, no risk for your connect. You know the shit is going to move. I'll even give you a cut off of each batch. I just need the connect," John says.

"I can't promise you that. John, once I'm out, I'm out completely. I'm leaving prison and that streets shit behind," Sherman says.

"So what about me? So what about Big Moe? What about Rakeys and Blue Eyes and all the homies you'll be leaving behind. Fuck us? Is that how you're going to go," John says in anger.

"I didn't say fuck nobody," Sherman says staring into his eyes.

John looks toward Sergeant Jackson as he approaches the gate from behind the guard's station. John sighs. He repeatedly opens and closes

*his hands. He sighs again. He
menacingly looks into Sherman's eyes.*

"Sherrrrrrrrrrman, you know what I
mean," John says controlling his tone.

"Cells will be opening in five minutes!
You Jail Birds have been locked down
for four days so I advise you to be on
your best behavior! Any shit gets started
in here... this block will go on permanent
lockdown. You'll get one hour rec every
other day. Won't be no need crying to
the Captain and the Warden because
this comes from them and not me! If it
was up to me, ya would take showers at
your sinks like you animals are use to.
Four minutes, assholes!" Yells Sergeant
Jackson.

"He needs that knife in his fucking
throat. He talks to ya like that all the
time," John says angrily.

"He's a wanna be cop," Sherman
replies.

"Man, these are grown men! Why you
talking to them like they fucking kids or

punks?" John shouts at Sergeant Jackson. Big Moe pauses as he looks down toward them.

Sergeant Jackson walks over to the gate. "Fuck you, Jail Bird! How you going to talk shit to me in my house! They should be questioning why your ass is on the compound and everybody else is locked down," Sergeant Jackson yells.

John immediately struts toward the gate that separates him from Sergeant Jackson. Sergeant Jackson is leaning on the gate. Big Moe briskly catches up with John. John is pointing one finger at the guard and secretly reaching for his shank in the back of his pants as he gets closer to Sergeant Jackson. Big Moe gently presses his palm down on John's hand and the shank. With his other hand, he grips John's shoulder. "No. No," Big Moe calmly whispers.

John stops inches away from the guard. "You talk that shit to these motherfuckers! I'm all convict, nigga," John screams.

"What in the fuck does that mean?" Sergeant Jackson screams back.

"It means I'm all man. I'll die before I tell on a motherfucker! And I'll kill any motherfucker that disrespects me! And bitch you just did," John barks.

"You're threatening me!? You're threatening me! Is that what you're doing? You're threatening me!" Sergeant Jackson screams in pure rage.

"You take it anyway you fucking want it," John says.

Sergeant Jackson smiles, "I thought so. You smell just like pussy. Get the fuck off my block."

Big Moe immediately bear hugs John from behind as he desperately tries to grab the knife. Then Big Moe continually turns his own body from side to side to prevent John from grabbing his knife since John couldn't reach his own. Big Moe lifts John off of his feet and carries him to the gate that lets them off of the tier. "Sarge, let us off of the tier.

Sergeant Jackson nods his approval and walks over to the switchboard. He shouts over his shoulder, "All of you get the hell off of my tier!"

Chapter 49

Sherman is being pat down by a guard in the back area where the prisoners enter before seeing their visitors. He spots Psycho sweeping the floor in the area. The guard taps Sherman indicating that he was done patting him down. "Your visitor is seated at table six. I'll let my relief know what time your visit started. Enjoy," the guard says as he goes and takes a seat at a desk near the inmate exit door.

Sherman nods his head toward Psycho after Psycho greeted him. Then he walks into the visiting room and sees Ella waiting. He scans the room for Loretta but doesn't see her. However he sees Slaughter House being passed a balloon of drugs under the table by his female visitor. He also sees three other prisoners with their visitors.

He stops at the table with his arms open and smiling. Ella doesn't smile or stand.

"Have a seat," she says firmly.

He looks puzzled. "I don't get no love? Where's my baby?" he says as he sits. He reaches out to grab her hands but she puts them in her lap. "Is she ok? What's wrong?" he says with genuine concern.

He glances over and sees Slaughter House walking over to the vending machine and drop the balloon into the trashcan.

"I don't believe you could be so cruel. I've sacrificed so much for you. Since we have been together, my focus has always been on you. I have been to hell and back for you. I had a child because you wanted one. I took out a second mortgage on my house to pay for your lawyer. I send you money every week. My daughter and I go without so you can be comfortable in here and you do this to me?" she says with tears streaming down her cheeks.

He reaches across the table for her but she leans all the way back in her chair. "Do what to you? I would never do anything to hurt you. You know that. I love you. I love being with you. I love everything about you. You're my wife," he says sadly.

She holds up the front of her left hand and wiggles her fingers. "Ain't no rings on my fingers. Ain't no rings on my damn fingers! You are not my husband. I am so stupid! You have been stringing my dumb ass along. No more, Sherman. No more. How could you disrespect me like this? You had her in my house. She hugged and kissed my damn baby!"

They don't notice Susan entering the visiting room from the inmate exit area. Sergeant Jackson is close behind her. They stop at the desk where the guard on duty is seated. The guard on duty stands and begins to take of his walkie-talkie and gathering his belongings in preparation to get off work. The officers begin to converse. Then Susan spots Sherman and Ella.

"Huh?" he says with a look of confusion.

"Uh, shit! I'm supposed to be the dumb one. I'm the one with the blinders on. So, don't play dumb, Sherman, that's the role you gave me! No more," she shouts.

"Shhhhh. Stop screaming. They'll end the visit," he pleads.

"Fuck you and this visit," she shouts before burying her face in her arms and crying.

He motions to stand. Susan steps in between them. "This visit is over. I told you, Sherman, ain't no more of this," Susan says threateningly.

Sherman and Ella stand as Sergeant Jackson and the other officer come and stand on opposite sides of Sherman.

"Is there a problem?" Sergeant Jackson barks.

"Naw," Sherman says.

"Yes. This visit is over. She is supposed to be banned from visiting for suspicion of smuggling drugs into the institution. Plus, she is being disruptive," Susan says.

"What?" Sherman barks.

"No you didn't! You brought the drugs in here," Ella shouts.

"Ain't nobody bring no fucking drugs in here!" Sherman barks as he pulls out his empty pockets and lifts his shirt.

During the commotion, Psycho pushes the trashcan that Slaughter House dropped the drugs into the inmate exit room.

The other guard grabs Ella gently by the arm.

"Get off of me!" Ella shouts.

Sergeant Jackson points to Sherman. "Don't. You know we have to search you both. You come with me and I'll search you."

"I don't have no drugs! She's not searching me! She's probably trying to plant something on me!" Ella screams.

"You can search me. I'll take a laxative or whatever. I don't have anything but don't let her search my wife," Sherman says calmly.

"Ok. We'll call the cops so they can dispatch a female to check her. Come with me, Mr. Ford," Sergeant Jackson says.

Psycho steps back into the visiting room. He pushes the trashcan back to its original location. Then he leans against the wall by the vending machine and stares at the commotion with his arms folded across his chest.

"You see this shit you got me in because you fucking her? Look at me, Sherman! They're treating me like they treat you. Look what you have done to me. I promise you, you will never hear or see me again," she says before falling completely apart.

Sherman motions to go towards her but Sergeant Jackson grabs him around his arms from behind. "No, Mr. Ford, lets go."

"Don't worry about anything, baby. You didn't do anything wrong," Sherman says pleadingly.

"Everything I've done since meeting you has been wrong," she says with a broken heart. She then looks Susan in her eyes, "You can keep fucking him. I'm done."

The other guard leads Ella out of the visiting room into the inmate exit area.

CHAPTER 50

The cell doors open. The prisoners slowly and cautiously file out onto the tier. Blue Eyes and Razor lock eyes as they exit the cell. Razor smiles and nods toward him. Blue Eyes frowns and walks toward him. Razor's smile turns into a surprised look. He spits two razors from his mouth into his hands and loosens his shoulders.

"Hey, Blue," Rakeys shouts. Blue Eyes pauses and slowly looks behind him toward Rakeys. "Come'er, Blue," Rakeys says with a warning in his tone.

Blue Eyes looks at Razor. Razor is staring at him. Bear walks up behind Razor. Bear looks at Razor and follows his stare down to Blue Eyes. Bear shakes his head no toward Blue Eyes.

"What? What does that mean?" Blue Eyes barks. The whole tier pauses and looks in both directions as Blue Eyes snatches two shanks from his waist. Other prisoners start ducking into whatever cell is near them. Rakeys starts walking swiftly toward Blue Eyes. He pulls his knife out.

Butch walks out of the cell just in time to press his hands against Blue Eyes' chest. "Hold up, Blue. You know you can't do this," Butch reminds him.

Rakeys notices that Bear steps in front of Razor and signals him to stop but he continues to glance in Blue Eyes' direction. Rakeys steps in front of Blue Eyes, "What the fuck are you doing, Little Crazy? You know the situation," Rakeys says.

"Man, that motherfucker smiling in my face like he is saying, 'Yea. We smashed your man.' Fuck dat, Cuzzo" Blue Eyes says.

"Did he say that to you?" Rakeys asks.

Blue Eyes lowers his head, "Naw, but I could read his mind, Cuzzo".

"So you're a mind reader?" Rakeys says humorously.

"Man, don't play with me like that, Cuzzo. They slaughtered my man. I can't let it go like that. He wouldn't let it go like that, Cuzzo, and you know he wouldn't," Blue Eyes complains.

"Yesterday wouldn't put Sherman at risk from going home. He wouldn't do that. He respected Sherman," Butch says.

"Hold on. Bear is walking this way," Rakeys says as he sees him approaching. "Butch, keep Blue under control. Let me go meet this dude before Blue Eyes stabs the man." Rakeys meets Bear halfway.

"What's up, bro? I thought we had an understanding that the beef was squashed. We don't want no beef with Blue or any of ya. We want peace. We all got too much to lose," Bear said politely.

"We understand. I'll talk to him. Is Razor cool with it being squashed or does he have an issue he wants to address with Blue?" Rakeys asks with a tone that says we can go to war if ya want to.

Bear holds up his palms. "Naw. He's cooling, bro. There's no kind of beef with any of my guys. He was only responding to what he felt was aggression. However, bro, I will make it clear to him that that's not Blue's intent. We respect all of ya. Lets live in peace, bro," Bear says.

Rakeys nods his head in agreement. Both men take several steps backwards away from each other before turning around and walking back to their friends.

"I don't trust those crackers. As soon as Sherman leaves, it's on. Fuck them other niggas," Rakeys says.

Blue Eyes smiles and puts his shanks away. Butch shakes his head in disbelief.

CHAPTER 51

Captain Dewitt and two female officers are seated across a long table facing Ella. Her elbows are on the table and her hands are buried in her unkempt hair. She is exhausted.

"I believe you have never smuggled drugs in here. However, I was informed that you accused my officer of sleeping with Mr. Ford. Why did you say that?" Captain Dewitt questions.

"I didn't say that. If I did, I must have done it out of frustration because she ended the visit. I don't know that woman. I mean, I seen her a few times in the visiting room," Ella says completely drained.

"So, you said that to get her fired?" Captain Dewitt asks.

"Yea," Ella replies looking at him with red dry eyes.

"Because she's sleeping with your man?" Captain Dewitt questions.

Ella continues to hold her head but tilts her neck sideways and looks at him. "What? Nooo. I felt she was overreacting by ending the visit so I overreacted. Can I go now? Please? I have to get home to my daughter," Ella asks.

He nods his approval and they all stand. "One more question," Captain Dewitt says.

She looks at him and smirks.

"So you're aware that Mr. Ford has made parole?" he says.

Her eyes widen in shock.

Captain Dewitt smiled. "Yes. He made parole two days ago. I guess whatever the argument was about started before he could share the good news. He'll be home maybe tomorrow or Friday but no later than next week for sure. I thought I would leave you with some good news," Captain Dewitt says.

"Good for him. I'm done," Ella snaps before walking out of the door.

CHAPTER 52

Susan stops at Sherman's cell with a stack of mail in her hands. Rakeys is seated on his top bunk reading a law book with three other law books open beside him. Sherman is wiping off his shoes with a rag. They both look up at her. She counts them and starts walking away.

"That was really fucked up what you did two days ago," Sherman says.

She pauses and looks back into the cell, "I told you what would happen. You created that situation. No, what's messed up is what she did. Now I am under investigation. I can't even work any of the cell blocks without a partner."

He walks over to the bars. "You did that to yourself. Why in the fuck would you go to my house and start this bullshit?" he says fuming.

"From what I heard that's not your home anymore. She doesn't even want you to be released to her home. I guess that kills your parole."

"You find that funny?" he says.

"I didn't say that. All I'm saying is she could care less about you. Now you can't even make parole because of her," she says.

"I already handled that," Sherman replies.

"How?" Susan says.

"It doesn't matter," he replies.

"If you need an address, let me know," she says remorsefully.

"I don't need shit from you," he says.

"Fuck you. I don't have to put up with this shit," she says tearfully.

"Is everything ok?" the officer behind the guard's gates asks.

She shakes her head. "I'm probably going to lose my job because of her and you could care less," she whispers to Sherman before walking off.

She heads down the tier counting prisoners and passing out mail. She makes her way through the showers and up the stairs to the second tier. She begins counting the men and passing out the mail. She stops six cells away from Psycho's cell.

Psycho is standing at his cell door trying to get a good view up the tier through the bars. He can't see anything but he can hear her talking to a prisoner. He looks up at Bear on the top bunk. His feet are dangling off of the bed and he's picking his nose.

"Stop that nasty shit and come here," Psycho says frowning.

She walks away from the cell and continues counting inmates while passing out mail. As she approaches the next cell, she is startled to see Bear and Pyscho standing in front of the bars.

"Step back. I need to count ya," she says frowning.

Bear leans his back against the wall and Psycho takes a few steps backwards.

"That was a very unfortunate situation in the visiting room the other day," Psycho says seriously.

"You can't believe everything you hear," she nonchalantly replies.

"I believe the nigger bitch," Psycho says as he steps closer to the bars.

"Good for you," she says before walking away.

Psycho looks at Bear and puts his hand on his shoulder, "Go on to the feds, Brother". Then he steps back and Bear starts thrusting the cell door back and forth until it snatches open. He steps onto the tier and looks into her frightened eyes.

"Get back in that cell," she screams.

He loosens his shoulders and neck and wiggles his fingers. She starts backing up until he starts walking toward her. She turns and sprints to the end of the tier where the metal fence separates them from the guard's area. The other guard is looking up at her as Bear appears. He spins her around. She immediately starts punching him as the other guard calls for backup. Bear punches her in the stomach. She drops to her knees. He wraps his hands around her neck and begins choking her. She swings wildly. He starts strangling her. Her arms drop to her side as he lifts her off of her feet by her neck. The other guard continues to stare in shock as her legs begin to shake while her body starts convulsing.

Bear looks her in her eyes as her eyes start to roll in the back of the eye-sockets. He spits in her face.

"I cast your soul into hell, nigger lover" he says.

CHAPTER 53

Sherman exits Two Block carrying a knitted laundry bag with stacks of all the mail he kept from Ella and Loretta. Sergeant Jackson follows him out of the building. They begin to walk up the sidewalk side by side. Sherman scans the compound and sees three men picking up trash around the compound. He sees the back of John by the kitchen but doesn't recognize him. However, John sees Sherman. There is another man by 4 Block and a third man near 1 Block.

"You finally made it out. Why didn't you get out yesterday with the Butch fellow?" Sergeant Jackson says.

"I had to do a change of address," Sherman says nonchalantly.

Now that you're out, what happens with the rest of your life?" Sergeant Jackson questions.

Sherman hunches his shoulders. "I'm going to take it one day at a time," Sherman replies.

John pulls out a shank and hides it behind the trash bag. He slowly starts following them.

"Mr. Ford, that's a bad move. You should have created a plan while you were here. The odds are against you out there," Sergeant Jackson says genuinely concerned.

"Now I'm Mr. Ford," Sherman says.

John's footsteps quicken.

"You guys know I only be joking. I try to make this place as miserable as possible for you guys so when you get out, you stay out. I'm so tired of coming to work and seeing a pool of men who look just like me. Some of ya are younger than my two sons. Then ya get here and just give up. Ya mad at the world, feeling sorry for yourselves, and so ya start killing each other. Killing each other isn't going to get you home any quicker. I think most of the men here want to commit suicide but are too scared to do it. To be honest, Mr. Ford, I'm scared as hell for my family that you're getting released.

Sherman stops. Sergeant Jackson stops. John halts.

"So you don't think I deserve to be free?" Sherman says with a bitter tone.

"Tell me what have you learned in here? Tell me the rehabilitation you received? You haven't attended religious services or anything. This facility doesn't make you work or go to school, but those opportunities exist. Which one have you enrolled in since being here? What detail have you worked since being here? Tell, Mr. Ford? I can bet my life on it that you are more dangerous now than when you entered this place. I've seen you snap a man's neck on that tier. Yes, I am afraid of you. Society should be afraid of you. Look me in my eyes and tell me why I should believe you won't go out here and commit another crime," Sergeant Jackson says.

Sherman starts walking back up the compound. "I don't have to prove shit to you. The parole board said that I am rehabilitated," Sherman says.

Sergeant Jackson starts walking. John walks faster.

"God knows I hope they were right," Sergeant Jackson says.

Sherman smirks. John's pace quickens.

"Well, Mr. Ford, I wish you all the best. I hope that I never see you again, in here and definitely not on the streets. I will pray once we part ways that God touches your heart and changes you before you walk out of these gates. I really hope there is someone or something out there that you are willing to live and do right for," Sergeant Jackson says.

"There is," Sherman says smiling to himself. John takes larger steps. He is within six footsteps away from them. He is close to the right shoulder of Sergeant

Jackson and the right shoulder of Sherman.

Sergeant Jackson pats Sherman on the shoulder, "Glad to hear it," he says sincerely. As he pulls his hands away, John stabs Sergeant Jackson on the right side of his neck. Sherman raises his left shoulder to shield his neck and gets scraped with the blade on his shoulder as John swiftly turns the knife on him. Sergeant Jackson grabs his neck. John refocuses back on Sergeant Jackson and stabs him across his face as the Sergeant tries to turn away. John plunges the blade into his side. The Sergeant stumbles and falls to the ground. John stabs the fighting Sergeant six more times in various spots on his upper and lower body until the Sergeant stops moving. Then he turns to Sherman who is slowly backing away.

"I should have made sure I finished this on The Hill. I knew I should have killed you the first day I saw you here. Oh well, I'll do it now. Sorry I have to ruin your plans to leave here alive," John says with a calm but menacing tone.

Sherman stops backing up. He stands his ground. John fakes like he is going to charge. Sherman doesn't move. John smiles and pulls out another shank with his free hand. Sherman just stands there. John fakes a thrust forward. He fakes again. He then moves swiftly toward Sherman with the knife in his left hand swinging horizontally and with a swift vertical thrust towards Sherman's midsection with the shank in his right hand. Sherman steps outside the blade in John's right hand and smacks him across the side of his face with the mail in his right hand before kicking him in his left hip. John stumbles forward from the kick but immediately slashes backwards with the blade in his left hand. The blade cuts Sherman across his left ankle. Sherman sends a right hook over John's right shoulder and pounds him across his cheek. John slides off of the punch and spins to his left as he slashes in Sherman's direction. The tip of the blade stabs Sherman down his chest. Sherman punches him with his left fist on the tip of his chin. John stumbles backwards. Sherman moves swiftly and kicks him under his right knee. John's body crashes to the ground. He immediately rolls to the left. Sherman starts stomping his ankles. John's upper body comes forward and he swings the shanks wildly. Sherman jumps backwards. John immediately gets up. Guards are starting to run toward them from all around the compound.

John shakes his shoulders as he smiles. He then charges at Sherman, swinging the shanks in opposite directions in front of him. Sherman crowns him on the top of his head with the mail and immediately punches John in the face with his free hand. John drops one of the knives as he stumbles backwards. The guards are still running toward them.

Sherman scoops up the shank as John charges him. Sherman instantly drops to his knees and clobbers him with the mail bag before stabbing him on the side of his right knee. John grips his knee in agony as Sherman jams the blade into John's temple. He yanks the blade out as John's body slumps to the ground. He moves toward John's upper body and stabs him twice in his adam's apple before the guards could reach them.

THE END

These are other projects and businesses of Lamont Carey:

Serving-N-Time

Serving-N-Time Is a pen pal company owned by Lamont Carey in support of connecting caring individuals with prisoners. Currently, there are over two million prisoners incarcerated. Over 85% of prisoners will be released one day. Our goal is to assist you in connecting and encouraging them through correspondence. Prison is a lonely and depressing place. It can completely break a person's spirit and leave them angry with the world. Rehabilitation has to begin at the core of the person and prisons don't take on this responsibility proactively. It is up to us, the society, that these individuals will return to by assisting them in changing and spending their time preparing themselves for release and living productive lives after prison. We don't want them to end up like K.T., Gangster, Brace, John, or Sherman.

Prisoners can change. I did.

It just takes a willing individual and a caring community to change a life. Do you care enough to make our world a better place by equipping people who have made mistakes with the decision making skills that you possess?

If you are interested, go to: www.servingntime.com and choose a prisoner to write today. Their picture and contact information is posted on the site.

If you are a prisoner that is looking for a way to connect with people who want you to succeed, contact us at:

Serving-N-Time
P.O. Box 64256
Washington, DC 20029

Send us a self addressed stamped envelope and we'll send you information on how to get your profile placed on our internet site.

IMAGINE CD

Lamont Carey's award winning CD containing such hits as "I Can't Read", "Confidence", "I Hate This Place", "She Says She Loves Me", and ten other electrifying spokenword pieces.

Laws Of The STREET-The Play (DVD)

Lamont Carey's playwriting directorial debut at the John F. Kennedy Center. It's a story about an inner city kid that takes the wrong path, leading to a life of murder.

Learning To Be A Mommy-The Play (DVD)

Lamont Carey's second play directed at the John F. Kennedy Center. A story about a young girl who struggles while making sure her family is safe, healthy, and protected. She has to make some choices that could leave her dead and her family destroyed.

Book version forthcoming.

Upcoming projects from Lamont Carey

Capers

A story about the relationships, struggles, and inner thoughts of three teenage friends who decides to rob a kingpin drug dealer and the war that quickly ensues when his crew finds out.

The System

A fictional story about the peer pressure of one man getting released from prison and trying to change his life for the better when his buddies are getting major money in the streets.

The Redeemer

A story about the anti-Christ coming into the world as Jesus Christ.

Laws Of The STREET

The novel series & TV series
A story about a community that is forced to
live under the rules set by the criminals.
This is a look into the lives of those who
want to escape, those who don't believe
their are other options, and those who like it
just the way things are.
(trailers available for viewing:
www.lacareyentertainment.com)

Outside The Gate

A documentary about the struggles,
strategies, and triumphs of four ex-
offenders who were determined to succeed.
Four different lives. Four different
successes.
(Trailers available for viewing:
www.lamontcarey.com)

Reach Into My Darkness. I Hate This Place

A collection of Lamont Carey's most
celebrated and socially driven poems, which
includes "I Can't Read", "She Says She

Loves Me", "The Streets Keep Calling me", and so much more.

The Business Side Of Spokenword

This book is a blueprint on to how to maximize your money making potential as an artist. It covers everything from protecting your material to securing performance opportunities.

Transition from prison to success

Is a self-help book about staying out of prison and living a successful life as a positive member of society.

Booking Lamont

Lamont Carey is not only an author, he is an international award-winning spokenword artist, filmmaker, playwright and motivational speaker.

To arrange to have Lamont Carey speak or perform at your next event anywhere in the world, contact LaCarey Management at: **lacareyentertainment@yahoo.com**

You may visit the website at:
www.lacareyentertainment.com
www.lamontcarey.com
FB: LaCarey Entertainment, LLC
Twitter: @lamontcarey

Send fan mail to:

LaCarey Entertainment, LLC
P.O. Box 64256
Washington, DC 20029